Praise

Roberta Bryer-King reminds us that God wants a passionate relationship with us. Too often, we focus on our faults, failings, and shortcoming as reasons why we delay or even push-back that relationship; we think we are not good enough to be loved by God. This book cuts through all of that and helps to focus on a life full of awe and wonder with a God who loves us far more than anything our failings can change.

—Kary Oberbrunner, author of *Unhackable,*
Day Job to Dream Job, and *Elixir Project*

In a world where so many are struggling with a great deal of fear, anxiety, worthlessness, and pain, along comes a much-needed and essential message of healing and hope. In *Embracing Your Wicked Good, God Awe-Full Life*, my friend, Roberta Bryer-King, gives us a practical roadmap on how to build a deep and genuine relationship with God that will give us the ultimate freedom from our struggles in this life. This is a must-read for everyone!

—Doug Fitzgerald, author of *ONESHOT.ONELIFE.*,
Best-Selling Author, Speaker, Life Coach & CEO

Roberta Bryer-King is a writer, not just an author. Her gift in communicating truth in story and prose is compelling. She delivers the most important lessons in life that will change your perspective forever: don't let your imperfections keep you from loving and doing all God intended you to do. This book is a must-have addition to your library.

—Sally Betters, author of *From Crisis to Compassion,*
Speaker, Certified Life Coach

In *Embracing Your Wicked Good, God Awe-Full Life,* Roberta Bryer-King delivers a beautifully written and encouraging book to help people let go of their shame and unworthiness in the process of being healed with, through, and in the love of their Creator. She then goes on to inspire you through her journey to have the courage to dive deep into your relationship with the One who loves you beyond measure. Accept God's invitation to dance with Him here in this life and all the way into eternity.

—Christina Semmens of Say Yes to Holiness; Speaker,
Spiritual Mentor, and
author of *Say Yes: Discovering Purpose, Peace
and Abundance in Daily Life*

This book is thoroughly enjoyable! In the freedom of one entirely unselfconscious, Roberta communicates the things she teaches about God by sharing as many well-told stories of her encounters with Him. Evidence of her relationship with God is found on each page, inspiring the reader to desire prayer and a greater intimacy with Him as well.

—Father Rob Ketcham, *petersboat.net*

EMBRACING YOUR WICKED GOOD, GOD AWE-FULL LIFE

Rejoicing in Your Imperfection, Letting God Heal
You, and Making Your Stumbles Part of the Dance

ROBERTA BRYER-KING

Printed in the United States of America

Published by Author Academy Elite
PO Box 43, Powell, OH 43035
www.AuthorAcademyElite.com

Identifiers:

Library of Congress Control Number: 2020916532

ISBN: 978-1-64746-474-5 (paperback)
ISBN: 978-1-64746-475-2 (hardback)
ISBN: 978-1-64746-476-9 (ebook)

Available in paperback, hardback, e-book, and audiobook

All Scripture quotations, unless otherwise indicated, are taken from the Holy Bible, New Revised Standard Version®, NRSV®. Copyright ©1989 Used by permission of The National Council of the Churches of Christ. All rights reserved worldwide. Bible verses italicized at author's discretion.

Any Internet addresses (websites, blogs, etc.) and telephone numbers printed in this book are offered as a resource. They are not intended in any way to be or imply an endorsement by Author Academy Elite, nor does Author Academy Elite vouch for the content of these sites and numbers for the life of this book.

To Those of Us Who Need the Courage to Dance

My imperfections and failures are as much a blessing from God as my successes and my talents and I lay them both at his feet.

—Mahatma Gandhi

Contents

Acknowledgments............................... xi

Introduction xiii

Part 1
Being Wicked Good—Rejoicing in Your Imperfection

Chapter 1: The Perfect Imperfect Role Model—
            Peter Rocks!...........................3

Chapter 2: The Great State of Imperfection—
            Smile! You Are a Mess (And It Is Okay)! ...13

Chapter 3: Our Imperfect Friendship with God—If
            You Were God, Would You Unfriend Me? ..37

Part 2
Being God Awe-Full—Letting God Heal You

Chapter 4: The Perfect Imperfect Friendship with
            God—Delivering a Very Different Type
            of Friend with Benefits 67

Chapter 5: His Love Will Change You—You Don't
Change You 83

Chapter 6: Shhhhh—God Is Talking to You—Can
You Hear Him? 99

Part 3

Embracing the Art of Imperfection—Making
Your Stumbles Part of the Dance

Chapter 7: Imperfecting Your Palette—Separating
Out the Black from the Bright and
Getting Rid of the Grey 115

Chapter 8: God, My Choreographer—The Everyday
Dance with God (Stumbles and All) 125

Impact 133

Five Things You Can Do Right Now 139

Reflection Questions 141

Recommended Resources 147

About the Author 149

Acknowledgments

I have been incredibly blessed with extraordinary people who have been willing to be my companions on my life's journey. I am lucky. These people have loved me through the worst of times (and the worst of me) and the best of times. This type of unconditional love is what life is all about, and I am so fortunate to have been the recipient of so much of this kind of infinite love, grace, mercy, and compassion.

I want to thank my husband, Jim, who has been my overflowing source of love, strength, and forgiveness throughout our years together. He has listened to me endlessly talk about writing a book. When I finally started the process, our lives turned ridiculously busy and chaotic. Thank you for helping me push through the madness of our day-to-day lives to complete the manuscript. My book would not be here without you. I will be forever grateful to you for your support in reaching this lifetime goal.

For my sons—Alexi, Nikita, and Misha—you are the lights of my life. I am so honored that God gave me the opportunity to be your mom. Believe it or not, your presence in my life has taught me more about the love of God than probably anything else. You are each amazing, and I am so excited to see how you will take this world by storm! I also want to thank you for the she-shed you built with your dad, so I would have a place to write in peace and quiet. What a beautiful place to create this book!

For my mom and dad, who always told me I could do anything and always, always, always had my back. I am so incredibly blessed to have you as my parents. Your support and unconditional love have been overwhelming. I am still working to be remotely as good of a parent to my kids as you have been to me. I thank God each and every day for you both.

For my sister, Cecilia, the best sister a girl could ever have. Throughout our lives, we have always known that we could count on each other. I derived so much strength from just knowing you would be there for me, Cel.

For my editor, Felicity Fox. Wow. Just wow. You have been my ultimate cheerleader through this whole process. Thanks for your insights, your boundless enthusiasm, and your endless patience. We did this!

And to the incredible friends I have met throughout the years. So many people have shown me God's love and mercy—there are too many to count. I have always been amazed at how loving people can be. There are so many good people in this world.

Whether you know it or not, if you have been part of my life, even in a small way, you have shown me a different facet of God's love and have been a crucial part of me writing this book.

Here it is! I love you all so very much!

Introduction

A green light on the dishwasher indicated the dishes ran through the wash cycle. Because the light was on, it appeared the dishes were washed. However, when I started to put them away, I noticed a weird hue on the glasses. It was a bluish/whitish light coating. I wondered if I had lost my mind or if I was seeing things? My middle-aged eyes led me astray before, like when I yelled, "I love you!" to a man standing far away whom I later discovered was *not* my husband. *Hmmm, how weird.* I tried to assure myself that I was not going crazy. I do not have OCD; however, I do notice details. Well, maybe I am semi-OCD, in denial, or perhaps I am simply hyper-observant. Maybe I am more Shawn Spencer from the TV show *Psyche* than Adrian Monk from *Monk*? But I digress. I told my boys to unload the dishwasher, and I let go of the fact there was a bizarre glaze on the dishes and went on with my day. All was going swimmingly.

Until later.

I went to grab a few cleaning supplies under the sink in the kitchen. When I opened the cabinet, I knew instantly what had happened—it was toilet bowl cleaner. The generic dishwashing liquid bottle I had purchased was almost identical to the toilet bowl cleaner bottle, which for reasons unbeknownst to me, had found its way underneath the kitchen sink. My sons helped me around the house, and apparently, they had put the toilet bowl cleaner under the sink and subsequently used it to clean our dishes in the dishwasher. This was yet another exciting moment in my life with my three Russian-adopted sons who are now typical teenagers. They often forget to really pay attention to what they are doing—that is, of course, unless it is plugged in or wears lipstick.

So, back to the dishes. Yuck. Seriously, super yuck! I felt like Lucy spazzing out after Snoopy kisses her on the lips.

I panicked and struggled to remember what was in the dishwasher and pulled the items from the cabinets: *these three glasses, these plates, these utensils.* I talked to myself as I darted back and forth across the kitchen, opening cupboards, and grabbing more items. The thought of this whole episode grossed me out. I wasn't confident in my memory of what was all in the dishwasher, so in the end, I rewashed pretty much everything in the kitchen.

So, what do dishes washed in toilet bowl cleaner have to do with our relationship with God? A lot.

I recently realized my relationship with God *seemed* like a relationship, just like my dishes *seemed* as though they were washed at first glance. My relationship with God looked solid from the outside, but something was not quite right. I went to church, told people I loved God, tried to be a decent person (failing miserably many times), and even majored in theology in college. But the peace, joy, and freedom everyone talks about seemed to elude me. Quite honestly, when I spoke to more and more people, peace, joy, and freedom eluded them as well. We all proclaimed our faith made a huge difference in our lives. However, when we dove more deeply into the current state of our friendships with God and were completely honest, it became very apparent that something was off. A glaze of muck surrounded our relationships. What were we missing?

In the book, *How God Changes Your Brain* by Andrew Newberg, MD, and Mark Robert Waldman, they found some fascinating facts about those of us who believe in God:[1]

- In one of the surveys, only one percent of the respondents felt that they had a direct, personal encounter with God. Most people tended to describe God in an intellectual, abstract manner.

- There was a study at Baylor University (co-facilitated with the Gallup organization) that found that Americans tend to look at God as one of four personalities: authoritarian, critical, distant, or benevolent. The results of this study showed that out of the group of believers, only 23% saw God as benevolent. 31% saw God as authoritarian (the highest), 16% as critical, and 24% as distant.[2]

So, I did not only imagine things. I was missing something, and so were a lot of other people. Less than a quarter of us see God as benevolent? Obviously, we were not in genuine relationships with our God because we cannot be in a life-giving relationship with a God who is authoritarian, critical, and/or

---

1   Andrew B. Newberg and Mark Robert Waldman, *How God Changes Your Brain: Breakthrough Findings from a Leading Neuroscientist* (New York, NY: Ballantine Books, 2010).

2   Christopher Bader, Kevin Dougherty, Paul Froese, Byron Johnson, F. Carson Mencken, Jerry Z. Park, and Rodney Stark, "American Piety in the 21st Century: New Insights to the Depth and Complexity of Religion in the U.S. Selected findings from the Baylor Religion Survey," (September 2006): http://www.baylor.edu/content/services/document.php/33304.pdf

distant. We somehow missed the Good News of the Gospel—unconditional love and forgiveness. It is almost as if many of us feel that our relationship with God is forced. We *should* have a relationship with Him, but we feel as though He causes us pain, is distant, or continuously judges us.

I know that, for me, there was shame and guilt about my imperfections and my failures. How could I not feel terrible about being one of the most impatient people on the planet? My sons *definitely* remind me of this on a pretty consistent basis. One day, one of my sons said, "Mom, I am so glad you are not a school teacher. You would not be good." Uh, yeah. He is right.

Somehow, I thought I was not doing enough of the right things to *deserve* a friendship with God. My relationship was in my head and not in my heart. I could not *feel* God. I had known Him all of my life, but I could not *feel* Him. I could not feel His love, His joy, His peace, or His freedom.

I have been intrigued by a handful of people in my life who have had unwavering relationships with God. No matter what was happening around them, they seemed centered and peaceful. They did not know a God who would take away the pain and chaos in their lives, but they knew one who would be right beside them through it all. Their relationships with Him were enough. His love was enough. They *felt* it, *knew* it, *trusted* it. Even though they were imperfect and their lives were a mess at times, God's love remained their focus—*always.*

Their relationships did not have a cloudy, murky haze on them as mine did. The bonds were clear, life-giving, loving, and peaceful. I hope that everyone who reads this book understands one thing with their heart and soul (not their head)—there is absolutely nothing you can do to make God love you less. There is also nothing you can do to make God love you more.

Knowing and feeling this love is sheer freedom. I fear that many of us do not fully accept this gift of love from our benevolent God. We feel as though our imperfections drive a massive wedge between our Creator and us. What if I told you that your imperfections actually lead you to a more genuine and profound relationship with God? What if we started building our friendship with Jesus or God and had Him work on our imperfections *for* us and not merely struggle with our flawed willpower all of the time? What if we allowed ourselves to feel loved, forgiven, and free? What would our lives look like then?

> What if I told you that your imperfections actually lead you to a more genuine and profound relationship with God?

What if we were a little wicked at times, good most of the time, and, with God's help, we are *wicked good* all the time? And that is God *awe-full!* ☺

The Bible tells the stories of so many women and men who, no matter how flawed, put their relationships with God as priorities over fixing everything that was wrong with them. Why did they do that? Because they knew that the closer they got to God and the more real their relationships were with God, the more He would change them. Not only that, but they knew they had a lot of talents and strengths God had given them, and they were determined not to let their shortcomings lessen the impact of their lives.

My favorite of all of these Biblical men and women is Peter. I want to be like Peter. After all, Jesus builds His church on Peter. He felt free to be himself, trusted in God's mercy, believed in his soul what God told him, and changed the world. The best part is he was a complete mess at times.

Let us start by looking at Peter's love for Jesus and Jesus' love for him even amid this famous Apostle's shortcomings. How did Peter allow Jesus to make his stumbles part of the dance?

Part I

BEING WICKED GOOD—REJOICING IN YOUR IMPERFECTION

••• | •••

The Perfect Imperfect Role Model—Peter Rocks!

That disciple whom Jesus loved said to Peter, "It is the Lord!" When Simon Peter heard that it was the Lord, he put on some clothes, for he was naked, and jumped into the sea. But the other disciples came in the boat, dragging the net full of fish, for they were not far from the land, only about a hundred yards off. When they had gone ashore, they saw a charcoal fire there, with fish on it, and bread.

—John 21:7-9

PETER *THREW HIMSELF* out of the boat, into the sea, and swam to Jesus. He did not wait. He did not jump into the water. He did not sit and think about it. He *threw* himself into the sea and swam to the shore. No one else on the boat had this kind of reaction to seeing Jesus. Peter could not contain the sheer joy and excitement he felt knowing Jesus was on the shore.

This scene on the Sea of Tiberias is one of the initial times Jesus appeared to the disciples after His Resurrection. According to the Scriptures, Peter had not yet had a discussion with Jesus to ask for forgiveness for denying Him three times prior to the Crucifixion. Yet Peter still threw himself into the sea and swam toward his Savior, knowing Jesus would welcome him with open arms. Peter knew Jesus loved him unconditionally and wholly forgave him. He felt it in his core.

I do not mean to sound sacrilegious, but when I read this passage in the Bible, I picture the reunion between me and my dog, Roo, after we have been away for a long time. As our family walks through the door, Roo's excitement is uncontainable. She wags her butt back and forth with such force; it makes her whole body shake—she is an Aussie with no tail. As she jumps up and down and runs in circles, she practically falls over.

Roo runs me over, licks me, smiles, barks, and acts happy and crazy. Her love is so immense, so overwhelming, so joyful. She is not angry that we left. She is so happy we are back—no questions, no conditions. Again, my aim is not to lessen Peter's love for Jesus by comparing it to my dog and me, but the visual image of Peter's reaction of utter joy, peace, excitement, and freedom is very similar. Peter saw Jesus and did not take even a second to think. He grabbed his cloak and threw himself into the sea. Deep in his soul, he was so connected and in love with Jesus and only wanted to be near Him again as soon as humanly possible. Peter did not worry about his sin, unworthiness, or shortcomings. He trusted Jesus fully and believed that Jesus was indeed who He said He was.

People in the Bible were as *human* and imperfect as we are today. Peter had not had a chance to talk to Jesus after he had denied Him three times before the crucifixion. Let me say that again—he disavowed the Son of the Creator of the Universe in person *three* times. In Matthew 16:23, *But he turned and said to Peter, "Get behind me, Satan! You are a stumbling block to me; for you are setting your mind not on divine things but on human things."* If you Google "Peter's mess-ups," there are a ton of articles about Peter's failures.

Yet, Peter *threw* himself out of the boat and *swam* to the shore.

He was not ashamed. Beyond any shadow of a doubt, he knew Jesus loved him. Jesus did not focus on these temporary failures. In John 21: 15-17, Jesus asks Peter three times whether he loves Him. Peter seems frustrated at Jesus for asking the same question over and over. Jesus wanted to heal Peter by asking Peter to proclaim his love for Him, one time for each of his denials to reassure Peter that He did indeed continue to love Peter and forgave him each time he disowned Him. Peter already felt this in his soul, and that is why he was so annoyed at Jesus for asking him all of these questions. This passage always brings to mind the scene from the *Princess Bride,* "Hello, my name is Inigo Montoya. You killed my father. Prepare to die."[3] The Count got so sick of Inigo saying the same thing so often so then he shouts, "Stop saying that!"

When I used to contemplate my *boat* story, I pictured myself sitting in a kayak as Jesus was at the shore. (I would never, ever think of myself in a fishing boat. I had a work teambuilding incident on a deep-sea fishing boat in Florida. Two words: vomit and coworker. Therefore, I choose kayaks for sea vessels in my contemplations.) Alone in the kayak, I gently paddled through the Scarborough Marsh, which is an absolutely beautiful tidal marsh near Portland, Maine. I paddled toward the Atlantic Ocean around sundown. It was beautiful to see the sky lit up with brilliant colors. The sound

---

3   Rob Reiner, *The Princess Bride* (1987; Santa Monica, CA: MGM Home Entertainment, 2007), DVD.

of the paddle rhythmically hitting the water put me in an almost trancelike state. When I opened my eyes, I saw Jesus on the shore, so I jumped into the water and swam toward Him.

Except that was not my story. In my old story, my stomach dropped when I saw Jesus, and my heart pounded. Instead of focusing on His love for me, I focused on all of my failures, sin, and feelings of unworthiness. I knew He loved me, but I panicked. Suddenly, I violently paddled against the incoming tide as my kayak slowly drifted backward toward Jesus, despite all my efforts to take my kayak in the opposite direction. Finally, the kayak wedged itself in the sand on the beach—*deep sigh*.

"So, like, hi, Jesus. Whatcha doin' here?" I tried to hide in the shell of the kayak with no luck. Face-to-face with Jesus, and I wanted to disappear due to my shame and disappointment. Slowly, I turned around to look at Jesus and wondered if He would smile or be mad. Would He hug me? Would He walk away? Could He really love me with all my imperfections and forgive all the messes in my life and love me unconditionally?

The overwhelming answer is yes!

He does not care what I did yesterday or what I am going to do tomorrow. Truly, He is thrilled I show up to be with Him. Because when I am with Him, He knows that I am willing to let Him change me. Once I finally realized this, I was eager to have a *real* relationship with Him.

When my husband and I adopted our kids from Russia, two of my three kids had very different reactions to our arrival to pick them up. In the Russian adoption process, adoptive parents have to go to Russia two or three times before bringing the children home, and there are months in between the trips. Therefore, after the kids meet you, you go away for a while. So, during our first visit in October, we told the kids we loved them and gave them three things to remember us: a picture book, a green fuzzy blanket, and a stuffed animal.

We were called back to Russia for our court date in December, and my husband and I thought that the kids were going to be so mad because they would not have understood why we had been gone for so long. And indeed, one of our kids was really mad. A few of his friends had been adopted by Russian families, which was a much faster process. Meanwhile, he waited for us to return after he had bragged to his friends at the orphanage how he had parents, but then we went away. He had been through trauma as a toddler and already struggled with separation. So, when he saw us, he was understandably upset. Even though we did not speak the same language, I heard the questions in his head. *So, where were you? Why were you gone for so long? Do you even really love me? What kind of people are you?* To be clear, I totally understand why a little kid would have this natural, normal reaction.

Many of us think God feels this way toward us when we try to engage in a relationship with Him (especially when we have been away for a little while). We think He will be cold, distant, confused, judgmental, and unforgiving in the way an angry human father might be. The point here is sometimes we expect God's reaction to be like my son's because we believe God cannot overlook our imperfections or the fact we have been distant for a while. We also assume God's cold and distant reaction will never change until we can prove we are perfect.

But God is 100% unconditional love; however, *we* can only show 100% unconditional love *some* of the time. God's love is so freeing if we would simply trust His Word that He loves us unconditionally. *"Come to me, all you that are weary and are carrying heavy burdens, and I will give you rest"* (Matthew 11:28) God did not say come to me, and I will judge you and reject you. On the contrary, He wants us to feel peace in His presence.

So, my older son embodied how I think God reacts to us when we show up to be with Him. My husband, Jim, and I showed up at his orphanage after two months of being away, and my eldest son saw us from across the room. His face lit up, and he threw down his toy and came running across the floor. He tried to avoid falling as he made his way through the obstacle course of other toys and books. "Mama! Papa! Mama! Papa!" When he wrapped his little arms around our legs, he would not let go except to get the picture book we made him, which was entirely worn out. It turns out he held it constantly and looked at the pictures and showed his friends his new family. He also slept with it every night. Did he care that we had been gone for a while? Honestly, I don't think it even crossed his mind at that moment. He was so glad we were there, and he wanted to be with us, talk to us, and play with us. My soon-to-be son did not care what sin we committed yesterday or if we were going to struggle tomorrow. All he wanted was to be present with us. There was no yesterday or tomorrow.

Does God love us all like this? Absolutely. But unfortunately, many of us do not accept that He does. And to be honest, I would think this would make Him very sad. Can you imagine if my husband and I rejected our son's love when he was so incredibly excited to see us? My son wore out his picture book thinking about being with us again! If we are honest, many times we reject that God is who He says He is. We reject His love for us and how much it can transform us.

There came the point in my life when I decided to trust God and accept His unconditional love for me. I stopped questioning it. It absolutely changed everything. Therefore, in my newer version of my kayak-on-the-water story, I paddle as fast as humanly possible to the shore. When I get there, I bowl over the Savior of my life like my dog, Roo, bowls over me, or as my one son ran toward me at the orphanage. Jesus loves me so much. I always knew that He loved me, but more importantly, now I can *feel* it.

Paradoxically, I believe because we stay so much in our heads, we begin to feel that something is wrong or *off*. We wholeheartedly know that God loves us and need to feel His love, yet our lack of letting ourselves causes us to sense something is wrong. Like my analogy of how I saw my dishes cleaned with toilet bowl cleaner vs. real dishwasher liquid, merely knowing God loved me in my head created a feeling of uneasiness. There was a *haze* that I could not put my finger on. My experience with God was supposed to be peaceful, freeing, and joyful. All I could feel was frustration, sadness, anger (sometimes), and disappointment. It was kind of like when I was excited to imagine the thrill of riding my first rollercoaster at Cedar Point. Instead, I walked off dizzy, terrorized, and very sick. The experience was not as I had envisioned. Yes, there were joyful times with God and times I felt loved, but I knew something more existed. In a nutshell, I thought I had to make an extraordinary effort of sacrifice and continuously strive to be a perfect person. All of this led to feelings of unworthiness, shame, and quite honestly, my strive for perfection led to nowhere. The worthiness game is a never-ending hamster wheel too many people never get off. This view takes away from the joy God is supposed to bring. God is about Good News, not suffocating news.

Was being loved by God supposed to be so much work with so little joy? When did my spirituality become so laser-focused on my sin and not on my relationship with God? How and when did I get into an invisible competition with everyone around me to see who would make the cut at the end of our lives? (And do not deny you think about that sometimes. We have a way of comparing ourselves to everyone. Yeah, I had my list of people I knew I would beat out and many more I thought would shoot right to heaven ahead of me.) Could God *really* love me in my sin? Was my relationship with Him more important than all of this?

At the end of the day, if I were candid with myself, I did not feel as if God truly loved me as much as I thought He should. I felt my imperfections were somehow stronger than His unconditional love. This sounds so dumb to write on paper, but it was true because I really and truly did not think God's love could penetrate through all of my mistakes. Or, if it could, it would be a joyous feat, not one of drudgery. Believe it or not, God is excited to help us work through the pain that causes us to make wrong decisions and sin. He wants to be our friend and does not hate us or want to make our lives miserable. On the contrary, He wants to heal us and be our friend, comforter, and source of joy.

So, how was I able to let go of my thinking and start to let those thoughts sink into my heart? How do I both know and feel in my heart and at the core of my soul that there is nothing I can do to make God love me less?

Well, I first needed to evaluate my current relationship with God, and I needed to be brutally and painfully honest. It was shallow. God was a good friend to me, but if I was truthful, I was a terrible friend. *OMG. God should have stopped texting me. He should have ghosted me, unfriended me, unadded me to Instagram, and lost His interest in my Pinterest.*

In the next chapter, I will examine this friendship from my perspective—or as close as I can get to that—of God's point of view. I think you will see there is so much peace and happiness God wants us to have if we would get out of our way and truly accept God for who He is. We need to quit making God into someone He is not and believe Him when he tells us who He is. Unfortunately, we are afraid to and continue to struggle. Why?

This brings me to another point. God is on our side. Really. Did you wince when you read that? Do we

God is on our side.

feel that as truth? How about this? God is wildly in love with us and was so happy the day we were born! Pondering both of these statements used to make me feel weird, uncomfortable, confused, and happy all at the same time. I know. It is a mish-mash of feelings that do not usually go together. I wanted to believe the statements, but my brain was like a brake. I wanted to believe, but I would not let myself accept God was on my side. But I do now. God thinks I am incredible (and you are too!), and He loves us on our worst and best days.

What does that have to do with anything? If God is on our side, He wants to help us. He wants to heal us so we do not do stupid, sinful things that eventually cause us more pain. Think about it. I know I have made the worst decisions when I have been hurt, sick, rejected, in pain, devastated, taken advantage of, lost, and the list goes on. People tend to make unwise decisions to hurt themselves or others unless and until they are at peace with God and feel worthy, as though they are on a solid foundation. We need to let God's awe-fullness into the parts of our lives where there is hurt and sin. He wants to restore us.

In reality, many of us have been doing everything back-ward. We have been relying on our fallible selves to fix the issues we have created. After we *fix* ourselves, we feel as though we can then engage in a loving relationship with God. This is futile. We never get to feeling that God loves us because there will *always* be something wrong and sinful in our lives. We need to be in a trusting and loving relationship with God *first*, and then we will change. He will change *us* in spite of ourselves when we engage with Him.

Once I saw how my thoughts were hindering my relation-ship with God, I realized I needed to be able to listen to Him. With all the craziness in our world, I needed to find blocks of time where there was *no noise* so I could hear Him. I needed silence and a lot of it. Good friends listen to each other, and I expected Him to listen to me, but I would not give Him the time of day. Any one-sided relationship will be unstable and shallow, and my friendship with God was genuinely lopsided, which was the source of my uneasiness and why I did not feel God's love. It was kind of like knowing you should love your spouse or best friend but never give them time to talk to you. Of course, you would have no idea how they honestly felt, and you would not feel the love from them. Time to listen is vital.

So, I became acutely aware of my every day and changed my priorities to make God at the top of the list. I also incorporated many different types of prayer in my day-to-day life. As we will later explore together, silence is the number one way to start feeling God's love for you. Your brain is wired to connect with God in silence and rewires to become more loving and empathetic when you meditate. God made your body and your brain to be able to communicate with Him. I will take you through some ideas on developing a deeper and more profound relationship with our Creator using various approaches to prayer.

When we can feel His love and let Him heal us and understand that He can make our stumbles part of the beautiful dance of life, we allow Him to create us into works of art. In the last chapters of the book, I take all these concepts and work to visually explain how all of this is intertwined. God and I are creating my life together every day. I am not working separately from him, trying to be perfect and hoping that He gives me an A. When my alarm goes off every morning and my feet hit the floor, I give every part of me—imperfections and all—to my Savior to mold, paint, or choreograph into something amazing that will positively impact the world for Him. He is my muse, and I am His.

··· 2 ···

The Great State of Imperfection—Smile! You Are a Mess (And It Is Okay)!

We are all wonderful, beautiful wrecks. That's what connects us—that we're all broken, all beautifully imperfect.

—Emilio Estevez

I AM IMPERFECT. Ask anyone who knows me. (Haha!)

As much as I hate to admit it, this has been one of the hardest things to acknowledge openly and wholeheartedly accept about myself. Everyone is flawed. However, there is a bewildering expectation from believers and non-believers that if you genuinely believe in God, you do not sin at all or hurt other people. And with that, God-fearing people do not hurt you. I am not sure about you, but I find this expectation absolutely irrational and yet so incredibly hard to shake. Why?

For those of us who have been in church for a while, it has been beaten into our heads that we need to get our stuff together. (I would put a stronger word in there, but I am trying desperately to stop swearing so much!) Only when we are all together are we godly people. Unfortunately, stopping our sinning is often presented as a prerequisite to developing a relationship with God. *We should fear God and get ourselves on the straight and narrow as soon as possible, or God does not really want anything to do with us (and we should be too ashamed to want to reach out to God in our less-than-ideal state).* In effect, we believe we are losers who do not deserve a relationship with God. This is what keeps people from coming to church, and it gives Christianity a bad name.

There seems to be significant confusion about a God who wants us to confess our sins and feel terrible—to the point of self-punishment—versus a God who wants to be in a relationship with us and heal us from the inside out, skipping the self-preservation spiral of shame. If we believe God to be an authority figure, like a cop, then we only think God is interested in us confessing our sins. It is as though God is following us around in a cruiser and shines a bright light into our face when we do something wrong. But God actually wants reconciliation too. He wants to join us in our journey of healing.

We all make mistakes, and somehow, even our Church focuses on shaming us. Why are we so addicted to feeling bad? What does all of this self-loathing get us? Nothing. I would suggest that it actually drives us away from God because we then look at God as someone who hates us and is perpetually disappointed with us. This attitude makes us spiral downward, which prevents us from tapping into the part of us most like God, our souls. With shame and loathing, we stay in a constant cycle of fighting our egos and somehow struggle to make that part of ourselves *right or redeemed*. We fight with our pride and end up in misery. It is futile because we will never truly *fix* ourselves. The more time we spend dwelling on how fallen we are, the less time we devote to the one thing that will make us well and make us free—our relationship with God. Only He can change us if we have a connection with Him. Self-loathing and shame shut that relationship off. I hardly have a prayer to become a more peaceful, loving, and free person if I focus on cutting off my relationship with God. I am not only doing a disservice to me but also to all those I could touch with God's love. I, in my own shame, am choosing to limit God's love in the world and His work in my life.

> I, in my own shame, am choosing to limit God's love in the world and His work in my life.

Wow. That really hit me hard when I thought through that. My ego and quest to be perfect took precedence over humbling myself, accepting God's forgiveness and joy, and forming a relationship with Him that could change me and change the world. I was causing my misery and limiting the love in my life.

So, if God can change all of us for the better and make our lives spectacular, why is there so much focus on *our* ability to fix our sin? I think it is because sin is something that can be measured and controlled (well, at least we think it can). This idea is ridiculous, but hear me out. If I act 100% in the right way, I must love God 100%. If I am only 50% holy, I must not really believe. I must only love God 50% (or less). I have it in my subconscious somewhere that I can only make it to heaven if I have an excellent score. So, I keep aiming for an exceptional score. In my corporate world experience, the saying goes, "You can only manage what you can measure."

(Pause)

Yeah, I am back. I had to go vomit when I heard that quote. It always reminds me of the movie *Office Space*.[4]

Anyway, is that true? If I sin and am imperfect, can I still be in love with God? Can God nonetheless be in love with me? Can I still be considered a virtuous person? What does this mean for my spiritual health?

I used to think that I could not really love God while being a sinner. Unfortunately, we have a lot of people in ministry leadership positions who tell us directly or indirectly that we need to be perfect, or we are out of luck. It is only when we get up to some standard that we will even be acceptable to be in church, for goodness sake.

Here is the equation for getting into heaven that I have constructed from 50 years of being a Christian and listening to a ton of homilies. Notice the parenthesis and the order of operations from when you were a kid in algebra class.

Ticket to heaven =
(Awesome acts of unconditional love + ½ (Average acts of goodness) + 1/8 (Grin and bear it acts of pseudo-niceness when it is all you can muster))
Divided by
(Big sins + 1/3 (Sins that are dumb) + 1/7 (Sins that you don't even know you did) + 0.0000007 (Sins to mean people – these don't count as much—lol))

All of this multiplied by the square root of 666. Kidding. (In case you did not know, 666 is the number associated with the devil.) The higher your ratio of selfless acts to those not so awesome gets you in the door. Oh, wait. What does the score have to be? Hmmm, no one seems to ever tell us that, but we always tend to be sure that our scores are never high enough.

---

4   Mike Judge, *Office Space* (1999; Beverly Hills, Calif: 20th Century Fox Home Entertainment, 2006), DVD.

Or we think it is something like this equation. I swear that if we are really honest with ourselves, we have some weird tally in our brains going on most days. The result is almost always, "Well, I am at least not as bad as Suzy. Her number of sins must be higher than mine." We look to the world to feel more secure in our destiny with God to lessen the fear that swells up in our hearts from time to time, telling us we are unworthy and will not make the cut. After all, everyone else has it all figured out, and we are left alone in the dark. How scary is it to think that we are continuously getting an F in our spiritual life? The consequences of failing are disastrous in our minds. God, that is a lot of pressure. Seriously, God, that is a lot of pressure!

Do we really and honestly think in our heart of hearts that Jesus died and left us an absurd math problem with an unknown and unattainable goal? That is the Good News? As I have been lured recently back into algebra problem-solving with my kids, there are answers to "x" in algebra. But there are no answers to the number of sins or good works to get us into heaven. Honestly, *there are no answers.* Why do we develop equations to solve problems that have no answers? More often than not, we use this ridiculous math to create the illusion that we are better than the people around us, and by God, *they* are all going into the fiery depths of hell way before we would ever get there. We keep taking deep breaths, trying to assure ourselves we are okay. We will make the cut.

This scenario reminds me of my golfing days. After playing golf as a kid on my high school team then captaining the women's golf team at the University of Notre Dame, I went on to play professionally on the mini-tours. I relate a lot of my life to my experiences with golf. In a professional tournament, we all put up a score, and some people got cut. But unlike golf, when you miss God's cut, you do not get paid and pack your bags and move on to the next tournament. You end up burning up for eternity, or so they tell us. Big stakes, to say the least.

Anyway, to sum up, this whole diatribe—this is dumb! And yes, I am yelling at me and everyone out there. Stop this! This pursuit of perfection does not embrace love, peace, freedom, grace, or anything that comes from God. And to make matters worse, we will never even know what some of the numbers in the equation are. Trust me, we all have sins we commit, which we do not even know about because our souls are unaware. How do we control the transgressions we do not know about? Is *being perfect* what all of this is really about? The answer to this question is no. We are forever imperfect humans. Demanding perfection from others and ourselves will make our lives miserable and despairing. There is no winning this battle of perfection and worthiness.

This is why the whole sin algorithm does not make sense. Depending on how deeply we have been wounded throughout our lives, we ourselves will not be able to heal all of the hurts that are the sources of our struggles. Based on the experience (or lack of experience) we have had with God as a child or as an adult, it is possible none of this will even make any sense.

Honestly, all of those so-called *sinners* in the Bible were not more sinful than the others; they were simply more aware of their sins. They knew they could not change without God. Everyone else thought they could do it by themselves, which is why Jesus always alluded to the fact that the *poor sinners* in the Bible had a leg up on the righteous people. Those identified as sinners knew they had to rely on God and reach out to Him, humble themselves, and look honestly at themselves in a mirror. Meanwhile, the righteous thought they had it all together and had the power to change by redeeming *themselves*.

We cannot *prove* to God that we are lovable. He is already madly in love with us. We will never be perfect, and people will always be able to point out our flaws. And even more importantly, morality is not the sole point of spirituality. Think about it. Atheists and agnostics can be moral and ethical. Laws have been put in place in our society, and many people's hearts are never changed. So, what does that really mean? Why do we want to be Christian? What is the Good News? God loves us regardless, and we can be with Him forever if we simply have a relationship with Him. I have this eternal relationship with a God who is crazy about me, flaws and all. It is Good News. It is *Great* News. The Creator of the Universe wants to hang out with me—His creation—and wants to mold me into an expression of Him, the best expression of Him I can be. And the closer I am to that, the closer I am to being who I am truly meant to be.

To become more loving, suffer less, and fix our shortcomings, we have to realize the path *starts* with forming a relationship with God. Our God is our Redeemer. I am not my redeemer. Unfortunately, many of us have taken the route of attempting to redeem ourselves and plan to notify God when we finish. That is alienating ourselves from God, and honestly, we are telling God that we do not need His help. *We are fine on our own, thank you.* It was very freeing to learn I am not my redeemer. God wants to create a connection with me to show me how to grow, how to get rid of suffering, how to be a better person for others, and how to be at peace. I cannot get this through self-help books and sheer willpower. I need to be able to hear God's voice in my soul.

I have changed my mindset to understand that life is a paper in constant draft form. We continuously rewrite it and improve it to get all of the nuances correct. Life is not a paper to turn in to God for a grade every day. Every day is dynamic with new challenges and opportunities. Our lives are such a blessing, and God wants to be part of that blessing. As Stuart Smalley says, "Progress, not perfection."

The State of Imperfection

What if we were good *and* bad? And what if that was okay? It is how God made us—Wicked Good.

So, how do we find any joy in this imperfection that we continually resist? More specifically, it is the state of being imperfect that is the blessing. It is not necessarily our short-comings—although God uses those as well. How in the world could being imperfect be awesome? How can it be a blessing? What is so great about being fallible all (or at least most of) the time?

You see, I think most of us fight this gift of imperfection. We see it as a drag, that something is insanely wrong with us. We do not consider imperfection for the sheer beautifulness that it is. We never would equate the term *joy* with it.

And do not misunderstand me. I am not saying that it is okay to go out into the world and sin as much as possible. I am merely making the point that God needs to heal us so we can be in a place to become more compassionate and more like Him. And as we know God more intimately, He will reveal to us more of our imperfections, which we can address together. We cannot change ourselves and then come to God. We will change *despite ourselves* when we spend time with Him. And all of these sins, struggles, and issues in our lives that come from pain and adversity will bring us closer to God and open us up to be more loving, empathetic, and compassionate to others. We can use our pain and struggles to heal others. We will find, over time, that none of life is really about us. We are here to show people God's love and let Him work through us, no matter what that looks like. Much of this is also focusing on letting go of our egos.

Let's look at some of the good things that come from the state of imperfection:

❖ **It draws us toward God to find peace, mercy, and love.** We get to experience unconditional love, grace, and forgiveness (which is God!). This was not an afterthought of God's plan, but it was part of it because it is who He is. We will not find perfect love through anyone or anything else on earth. We have to fall into the loving arms of our Creator to find pure, unconditional love.

❖ **It takes the heat off—there is no equation.** (If you have ever watched *The Matrix*, there is no spoon.[5]) We are not in competition. We are not perfect and never will be. We cannot fully heal ourselves—God has to do the healing. We have to let Him.

❖ **It frees us to look at others with compassion.** They are hurting. This is not some big contest but an awareness that we are all in pain and looking for kindness and healing. We can accept others who are hurting and help restore them instead of hating them or judging them. The root of most suffering and missteps is pain, and to root out this suffering, we need to root out our pain.

❖ **It causes us to become spiritually mature and form a relationship with God.** This relationship transcends our day-to-day imperfections and trusts that God will use all of it. We have to trust God and rely on Him. We are not creating our own religion and depending on our ability to be perfect. Instead, we count on God's perfection to help us. This whole spiritual thing is about God; it is not about us.

---

5   Andy Wachowski and Larry Wachowski, *The Matrix* (1999; Burbank, CA: Warner Home Video, 2003), DVD.

So, when did imperfection become ugly? As I sit here and write, I am looking out into a forest of all different trees. Some trees are crooked; some have moss; some are dying; some are on the ground and are already dead. Imperfect? Yes. Beautiful? Absolutely. My husband and I took a painting class at our local wine and paint bar, and there were a bunch of us painting the same picture. All the finished pieces of art were incredible. Moving. Different. They each had the perspective of the artists. Some of the people even went outside-the-box and added a flair to the paintings. Were they wrong? We could tell some people did not have an ounce of artistic skill, but we thought their landscapes showed honesty and simplicity—still artwork, still beautiful. Who is the judge as to what is perfect?

I can hear some of you now. Trees and paintings cannot sin, but we can. Some of our sins are way more than mere imperfections.

It is sometimes challenging to distinguish the difference between sin and imperfection. Sometimes imperfection does not involve deliberate wrongdoing, but sometimes it does. The problem I see many of us dealing with is the constant focus on all that is wrong with us. We focus on the little mistakes, the human errors, the forgetfulness, the medium-sized missteps, and the humongous errors in our lives. Then, we lump everything together into one giant ball of *OMG. I am such an awful person.*

Yes, we are imperfect. I forget where my keys are all the time. I forget to fill out forms at my kids' schools until after the due dates. I really do not like to play board (bored?) games with my family, and they know it. These are just about .00001% of my human imperfections, but they are not sins. And then there is my sin, which is my imperfection on steroids. These are the things I deliberately do or am unaware I do, which hurt me or others. I will not bore you with listing these out. 😊

We resist and punish ourselves for our imperfections, which are not sins, and we refuse to believe God can take the inadequacy and pain that produces sin and make it into something amazing. God's job, if we let Him, is to redeem our sin. That is indeed Good News!

Drawing You Toward God—Longing for Unconditional Love

> *True homecoming is choosing the way of Jesus, where we acknowledge the good and painful in our lives, and we ask for patience and courage to forgive all those who have wounded us on the journey. Their love was limited and conditional, but it set us in search of that unconditional, unlimited love. This way takes us on a path through the desert of suffering to our hidden wholeness and to our utter beauty in the eyes of the One we name God.*

—Henry Nouwen

There are many reasons to rejoice in our fallibility. The first and most important blessing is it brings us toward God. It literally pushes us into having a relationship with Him to find our happiness, peace, and love. We cannot find true unconditional love, mercy, forgiveness, and peace outside of our relationship with the Divine. Why? Because we and everyone around us are imperfect. We are drawn to the perfect friend, God. And as we will talk about a little later, this relationship with God allows us to heal from our core.

If you think about it, God's consistent, unconditional love is precisely what makes it so incredibly powerful and moving and draws us to Him. We also see glimpses of this unconditional love between imperfect people here on earth. Think about the moments when you have felt the most love. Or think about the feel-good stories in the media. What moved you? I get very moved when people show a love that goes way above and beyond, like forgiving others for horrible things, loving each other despite great tragedy and hardship, and giving to others they do not even know. The list is endless. Take a minute and think of the stories in your life or others' lives that move you the most, make you cry, make you smile, and put your trust back into humanity. Most of these stories involve some kind of unconditional love, rising above our human tendency to put conditions on everything.

One of the more inspirational stories I have experienced is the death of my husband's brother, Rick, and their family's response to the tragedy. I had heard rumors of this merciful family before meeting Jim and was in awe of their ability to forgive.

Jim and I went to the movie theater to see *The Shawshank Redemption* when it was initially released (yes, I am old). When the movie started, I noticed Jim had an absolutely horrified look on his face. He choked back tears and said, "OMG. That is the Mansfield Reformatory." *Okay, and what does that mean?* "That is where we used to go visit the man who killed my brother to share the love of Jesus with him and help him move through the guilt and shame and believe in His forgiveness." *Wow.*

Jim was only ten when he was home one night with his brother, Rick. Rick was about 22 at the time. They lived in a sleepy suburban section of Akron, Ohio. The rest of the family was on vacation and due to arrive back home. Rick heard some noises in the garage and went to investigate what was going on out there. He saw a man rummaging through the garage and chased him down the street. As they ran, the man turned around and shot Rick. Jim's parents came home later the following day, and everyone learned that Rick had died. Jim's parents, Russ and Kathy, who had not been very spiritual people for most of their lives, called the family together to pray. They thanked God for Rick and asked God to keep them from feelings of anger and revenge and to use the situation to glorify Him somehow.

For a few years, they did not know who killed Rick. Then, one day, a friend of the perpetrator turned him in to the police. The perpetrator was overcome with shame about the murder and to assuage his guilt, his friend thought it best to face what he had done. Now, the King family knew who killed their son. To make a very long story short, he was sentenced and sent to the Ohio State Reformatory in Mansfield, OH. It was there that Jim went with his parents to bring the Good News to this gentleman who had made an enormous mistake. They visited often, so Jim knew that prison very well. He remembered all of it as *Shawshank Redemption* unfolded on the big screen.

The prisoner they visited in Mansfield thought all of the King's family visits were insincere and some kind of ploy at first. It was Jim, as a young boy, who told him that God loved him even though he killed his brother. This moment seemed to change the prisoner, who was amazed at the mercy being shown him. He was eventually paroled from the penitentiary with the King's family's blessings, and he is a productive member of society.

If all of us are imperfect, conditionally loving people can have moments of grace like this as we let God work through us, how much more does God love us unconditionally?

We can show glimpses of God's unconditional love when we let Him work through us. Unfortunately, we are not consistent with all of this. For every story like the King family's response to their son's death, there are stories in our lives of unforgiveness, hate, grudges, etc. We are all inconsistent in our conditional loving of others. And the inconsistency of love can lead to pain. God cannot create pain in our lives because He never loves us conditionally.

> God cannot create pain in our lives because He never loves us conditionally.

If we were not imperfect and if the world was not flawed, we would not feel this unconditional love. We would not know the power of forgiveness nor the humbleness of knowing God's grace and mercy. God is unconditional love. I dare say we would not really know God if we did not experience His unconditional love that blankets our imperfections. My friends, that is a big enough reason to rejoice in our state of imperfection. God's unconditional love includes unconditional mercy, grace, and forgiveness. It is all part of the package, *real* love. And it is only in this state of helplessness and powerlessness that we experience the reality and meaning of grace. Grace is God giving Himself to us. When we reject this, we reject God.

Just think, if we were all perfect, we would not need an all-loving God. We would not need anyone at all, really. Would we need people to lean on? Nope. Would we need to be reflective at all? Nope. Already perfect. Would we need to pray? Nope. We would have it all under control. Honestly, if we were unable to experience God's unconditional love as imperfect people, what an unmarkable life that would be.

The mere fact that we are imperfect at our core creates a reliance on God. We cannot do everything ourselves. We have a longing for our Creator, for our God to make us whole and heal us. When we separate ourselves from our Creator, we become a lesser version of ourselves. However, God is never-changing. How could our sin anger God or change His relationship with us? I honestly hate the theory that we break our relationship with God when we sin. (I know I am going out on a limb here.) I know it does not make God overjoyed when we sin. However, we still have a relationship with Him. We move away from Him, but He stays. He still loves us unconditionally, and we will always be able to return to Him.

Take the Heat Off—There Is No Spoon

Do not try and bend the spoon, that's impossible. Instead, only try to realize the truth...there is no spoon. Then you'll see that it is not the spoon that bends, it is only yourself.

—Spoon Boy to Neo, *The Matrix*

I am not a fan of science fiction movies, but with three boys at home and a geeky husband, I have seen my share of Star Wars, Star Trek, and Avengers. However, I did really enjoy the 1999 movie *The Matrix*.[6] There is a scene in the film when the main character, Neo, went to see the Oracle, who is supposed to tell him if he was "The One." In the waiting room, the spoon boy shows up. This spoon boy is holding a regular spoon in his hand, and it is miraculously bending back and forth. The first inclination that people have while watching the movie is the spoon boy is bending the spoon with his mind. However, the boy eventually lets Neo in on the secret—there is no spoon. It is not the spoon that bends but us and how we think.

When I started to understand that our ability to have a relationship with God and be in heaven with Him when we die does not rely solely on the sin competition, it felt like a huge weight had been lifted. I found I struggled to *bend a spoon* by working to become the perfect person, a person who behaved better than anyone else. When I accepted that this was not the basis of my relationship with God and that there was no equation, it was then that I saw there is so much more to spirituality than all of this—there is no spoon at all. I focused on trying to master something that was not even there, which took my attention away from other things that

---

6   *The Matrix*

were much more important, like connecting with God and showing His love to other people.

We selfishly focus on ourselves when we sit in a spiral of doom and worry about our ability to make it to heaven. We should get out in the world and share how awesome God is. He loves us no matter what or where we are in life. People need to hear that message and reassurance that God loves them, regardless of their past actions or mistakes. When we know we are loved, God can use this to change us to serve His purpose for our lives. People need to know that we love them, and God loves them.

We need to focus on God, not our performance. Thomas Aquinas once said, "Man cannot live without joy; therefore, when he is deprived of true spiritual joys, it is necessary that he become addicted to carnal pleasures." When we focus on fear, we let fear dissipate our energy to love, and we are distracted by sin. Instead, we need to invest our energy in trusting God and singing His joyful song. Years of worry and fear have left all of us vulnerable to sin, pain, and suffering. We need to trust that God's love changes us, and we can trust this love. It will lift us out of despair and heal our wounds.

Seeing Sin as Pain—Offering Compassion to Others

Compassion will cure more sins than condemnation.

—Henry Ward Beecher

I have been blessed to have had the opportunity to watch the series *Broken* on the BBC.[7] It is such a deep, dark, yet realistic show about a priest in England trying to help his parishioners deal with the incredibly difficult circumstances of life. Some of the episodes include 1) someone pretended her mom was still alive to get retirement money because she was in poverty, 2) a woman gambled all of her money away and was suicidal, 3) a mother who dealt with the tragedy of her special needs child who was shot by the police. These are three of many other episodes not for the faint of heart, and it is definitely not a *feel-good* Saturday date night show. It is more of a shockingly reflective series that shows at a terrifying level how everyone struggles. Everyone has issues with pain, shame, guilt, etc. We are all broken.

Yet, for some reason, we think certain people can escape human brokenness, and we are jealous of them. Whether people admit it or deny it, we are all human and experience periods of pain. I have heard stories of people who claim their lives are free from pain, and I honestly do not believe it. At the very least, when loved ones pass away, people feel lost, hurt, and in pain. I would be absolutely amazed if a person can skate through life with no wounds.

One of the many insights I have taken away from *Broken* is the fact that broken people can help other broken people.

---

7   *Broken*. Directed by Ashley Pearce and Noreen Kershaw. Written by Jimmy McGovern. BBC, 2017.

We are all on this journey together and can help one another. Somehow, when we know others struggle too, it gives us a sense of normalcy in our battles. It continues to blow my mind that people think there are perfect people with perfect lives. Maybe it is social media, or perhaps many people hide their struggles in a Christian church. Therefore, some sins are not as public. Whatever it is and whatever level we experience it, we all experience pain, which leads us to sin. In the movie *The Princess Bride, Westley says it well,* "Life is pain, Highness. Anyone who says differently is selling something."[8] When you find pain, you find sin if you do not know how to deal with it.

It can be redemptive for others when they see our strong friendship with God and our willingness to share our pain. By others witnessing our struggles and failures, they receive hope that they are not alone.

Instead of beating people down (including ourselves) because we sin, we need to find the source of our pain and desperation. When we share the source of the pain with God, we can start to bring to light the behaviors the pain causes, and we can work with God to address them. Jesus came to free us from many of the things that cause us pain—worldly desires, lack of love, shame, lack of forgiveness/grace/mercy, etc. He taught us that we will always be loved, and we do not really need anything on this earth. If we are indifferent to the circumstances in our lives and rely on God's love to get us through, we can move through the pain. It will still be there, but we can work through it. We have hope. We have a purpose. We have love.

---

8   *The Princess Bride*

We are More Than Our Actions—Our Relationship with God Transcends Everything

God already loves us. He has no choice. It's as if we cannot get away from Him.

— Me

Many times in the Bible, the writers refer to God adopting us. I have always been uncomfortable with the adoption analogy. After all, we are all God's sons and daughters. Well, I guess I should say that at first, I was uncomfortable with the adoption concept until I adopted my three Russian sons. Then, I understood more of what the Biblical writers were talking about.

Like my kids taught me, there is not much of a life to lead when orphaned and alone.

When our kids arrived in the U.S. on Christmas Day 2006, we settled into our day-to-day living. It was quickly apparent these kids had never really known attention and love. We knew about the hernias—two of them had developed these hernias from crying so much. No one responded to the crying for years in the orphanages. Soon, we found out about scabies and parasites in their digestive tracks, the sicknesses, the underdevelopment, the lazy eyes, and the lags in learning. But over the next few months after coming home, we saw many more manifestations from the lack of a consistently loving environment.

Unfortunately, when we started our journey from Moscow to bring the kids home, I was very sick. I boarded the plane at the Sheremetyevo International Airport after vomiting multiple times in the bathroom. It was Christmas Day, and I was as sick as a dog. I had three little ones—Alexi (5), Nikita (3), and Misha (2). They all needed my full attention. I thought I could get a break on the plane. They would be watching TV in their seats and interacting with their dad. But we ended up on probably the only flight between Moscow and Paris with absolutely no entertainment. And then, as luck would have it, we were on the lone aircraft from Paris to New York with— you guessed it—absolutely no entertainment. The stacks of stickers and coloring books did nothing to interest these kids. They had never seen anything like them before. Needless to say, I arrived in the Cleveland Airport with our new family absolutely drained, exhausted, nauseous, and scared to death.

All the books on international adoption warn new adoptive parents to make sure that no other friends or family members meet the kids for a month or so while the kids get used to the parents as their new family. It is affectionately called "nesting."

Screw that. ☺ Hell, Het. ("No" in Russian.) My parents picked us up from the airport, and we also met up with Jim's parents. I went to the doctor the next day and found out I had both strep and the flu. Jim was *lucky enough* to end up with only strep. We were both sick and tired and had unruly children who only spoke Russian, running and screaming around the house—with scabies and parasites. My mom and mother-in-law spent days with us, washing all the bedding every night while we worked to eradicate scabies. And I mean *all* the bedding—the sheets, comforters, pillows, stuffed animals, etc. My dad and father-in-law ran errands for us. God Bless them all.

On the second night at home, I heard a noise in the middle of the night. It was a rhythmic, creaking noise that seemed somewhat rushed and stressed. I snuck out of the nasty sick corner of my bed and walked down the hall. My youngest was on his knees on his bed, rocking himself to sleep. My heart sank. Here was a two-year-old rocking himself to sleep. He had not had anyone rock him to sleep before.

As the days went on, we saw the kids stuff their faces at meals to ensure they had enough food and that no one would steal the food they had. They put so much food in their puffy cheeks they could not even chew. I kept worrying one of them was going to choke to death. The boys also each vied for our attention. They would not even acknowledge that the other brothers existed except to fight for one thing or another. When they played with toys, and as they reached for a new toy, they would not let go of the toy they just played with. The boys were so afraid that someone would steal it. They had tantrums, hit us, and bit us.

Our oldest had spent a few years in multiple hospital wards and moved from orphanage to orphanage. When Alexi had lived with us for eight months, he thought he would eventually move on. After all, this was the pattern he was used to in his life in Russia—hospital to hospital, orphanage to orphanage. It was only fitting that he thought he would have to move from family to family in the US. He felt his next family lived at the school, and he did not believe me that he was not going to move into the local elementary school after he had been going there for a few weeks. One night, I had to drive him to the school at 10:30 p.m. to prove to him that no one lived there. He did not really believe that he had a place anywhere and did not think that a family would love him.

What did these kids need to be able to relax and calm down? They needed to know they were loved and would be loved every day. Jim and I needed to be a constant in their lives to the best of our abilities. Through the years, they tested us to see just how far our unconditional love would go. It is more profound than I ever thought it would be. But for me, I could not have been that constant rock in their lives if I did not have a continuous foundation in mine. Yes, my husband is incredible, but both of us needed the ultimate unconditional love, God.

There were some days when I was on the floor in a fetal position, wondering how I was even going to be up to the task of being a mom to these kids. There were days when I was so exhausted, so defeated, and so overwhelmed I was inconsolable. (And by the way, I still have many of these moments!) I wondered how I was going to make it through the day-to-day challenges. As I messed up a lot along the way with impatience and yelling, (Was my voice really that loud?) I was not who I wanted to be. But I needed to dig deep and continue to love these kids even as we all struggled and made lots of mistakes. Does this sound familiar? It should. God does this. He continues to love us through all of our shortcomings.

But the kids had to take a chance and trust us. They had to make that leap of faith that we were not going to abandon them. There was nothing they could do to make us love them less; there was nothing they could do to make us love them more. We loved them—period—even when they were unruly, and we struggled to live up to what we felt was ideal. But we kept going to God to find that constant love and to give all of this over to Him.

And then, our sons started to change. The kids grew less stressed. The tantrums lessened. They did not hoard food or toys and slept through the night. Their faces wore smiles more often, and they played and joked more. A massive weight lifted off their shoulders. Because they were loved, they grew more peaceful and happy.

This is the same transformational love that Jesus has for us. He takes us where we are, looks to comfort us and heal us from our hurts—the lack of love and bad behaviors—and He catches us if we trust Him to be there. But we need to let go, and we need to believe in Him. The longer we resist this and think we are unlovable, the more our life spirals out of control with things like alcohol, food, drug addictions, and immoral behavior. When we feel shame, we do not go out into the world and do what God wants us to do—love others.

Unfortunately, our church has made it so incredibly challenging to feel lovable. It is as if they come to *our* orphanage and tell us to get our *stuff* (I so want to use another word) together, and when that happens, *then* we are lovable and can be adopted by God. Instead, we need to let *God* take us out of the proverbial orphanage and let Him love us and trust that love to eliminate our protective behaviors. Just like my kids could not suddenly stop hoarding or rocking themselves to sleep, they needed to be shown love and forgiveness and understand they did not need to worry. When they knew they were loved, it changed them. Jim and I never stopped loving them. Through all of the tears, frustration, fights, and anger, we never walked away. And day-by-day, things got more comfortable for them. They knew we were not going anywhere. We never will, and God is not going anywhere. He has so much compassion and wants us to let Him love us. He hurts when we choose to think we are unlovable. That is the furthest thing from God's mind. He made us lovable in the same way He is lovable.

Our soul—our lovable core—speaks directly to Him. He wants to heal everything preventing us from being happy and from being focused on love and life. He knows we are miserable when we are hurt. We do stupid things and sin, and then we have consequences. He wants to free us from all of that. Even while living through the effects of sin, He continues to love us. It is as if we cannot get away from Him.

Just like the sun, we cannot get away from God's love, and it does not change. It shines as brightly on the evil as it does the good. God's love is ready for us to accept. It remains there, no matter our decision. We simply have to realize that every day is an opportunity to choose to be loved. Fear is from us, not from God. God already loves us. He has no choice. He is and will forever be unconditional love. We need to decide to accept the incredible gift of love and run with it.

••• 3 •••

Our Imperfect Friendship with God—If You Were God, Would You Unfriend Me?

Falling in Love – Nothing is more practical than finding God, that is, than falling in love in a quite absolute, final way. What you are in love with, what seizes your imagination, will affect everything. It will decide what will get you out of bed in the morning, what you do with your evening, how you spend your weekend, what you read, who you know, what breaks your heart, and what amazes you with joy and gratitude. Fall in love, stay in love, and it will decide everything.

—Pedro Arrupe, SJ

WHEN I WAS in middle school, I had a mad crush on a boy. I will call him "Joe Smith." I remember writing "Mr. and Mrs. Joe Smith, Joe and Bert Smith, Joe Smith and Roberta Smith," and others down pages and pages of notebook paper. And the hearts. Oh, there were hearts. I thought of him all day at school. Then, Valentine's Day came, and I gave him a Valentine. I was so excited. Surely, he thought of me as much as I thought of him. First. Big. Rejection.

In some sense, God's loving us is similar to having a crush on someone who, for some reason, does not like us back. God is insanely in love with us. He has a mad *crush* on us and thinks about us all day. (Yes, I understand that His love is much more than a crush, but stay with me here.) He keeps trying to tell us he loves us through the silence, friends, sunsets, nature, and our lives, and we keep telling Him it is not enough. We do not spend time with Him and cannot love Him until He lives up to our expectations, or we meet our own expectations. When we are not confident in our relationship with God, we do not believe we are loved, and we do everything on the planet to distract ourselves from this. We reject the love of God.

And what else do we do when we are not confident in a human crush and do not know whether the object of our affection likes us? OMG! We act so weird around them and guard ourselves. I know that I get very timid because I do not know where the other person stands. And when we find out the other person likes us, the floodgates open. It is freeing and validating to be ourselves finally. There is significant relief there. God really does love us. We need to start to believe that so we stop acting so weird in our faith. Please do not be that awkward middle school kid wondering if God likes you. 😊

So, knowing that God likes me, do my actions show God that I like Him back?

Yes ☐   No ☐   Maybe ☐

Many of us focus on our friendship with God through our side of the relationship and what God does for us—He loves us and brings us peace, etc. He loves us, period—there is no comma. (Well, there was a comma in that last sentence, but God does love you. Period.)

But what about looking at our friendship with God from His perspective? How are we doing being His friend? How are we responding to His love? Do we really trust Him? Have we fallen in love with God? To make a real impact in the world, we need to believe what He says is true.

Becoming God's BFF – Do We Pass the Test?

I do not call you servants any longer, because the servant does not know what the master is doing; but I have called you friends, because I have made known to you everything that I have heard from my Father.

—John 15:15

To be quite honest, the whole idea of God being my friend was odd in the beginning. But what is even more bizarre is for me to be God's best friend. Really? Can I do that? He is the Creator of the Universe, after all. Why does He need us all to be His besties?

We owe it to God and ourselves to spend time with Him so His love can change the world. Because so many people are in pain, we can spread the Good News. God needs us to accept His love so we can heal others as He has healed us. We need to bear witness to the Light. *"But to all who received him, who believed in his name, he gave power to become children of God"* (John 1:12).

God needs us to accept His love so we can heal others as He has healed us.

But back to our relationship with God. I took a few months and examined the status of my relationship with God. How good of a friend was I to Him? Hang onto your seats, people. This turned out pretty ugly when I was ruthlessly honest with myself. I am almost too embarrassed to tell you all of this, but I think it will be helpful and possibly enlightening to many of you. And don't judge me. 😊 I will explain.

I loved God since I was a little girl, but I truly was a terribly inadequate friend to God:

- **TRUST**—I did not truly believe everything He said in the Bible. At the end of the day, I thought He was a liar if I was honest with myself. Love me, unconditionally? Hmmm, I could not believe that. Forgive me? Not 100% sure of that either. Did I trust that He would take care of me (whatever that really entailed)? Uh, no. I was a worry monger.

- **HONESTY**—I hid/shut Him out. I was purposefully not admitting my faults to God because I did not want Him to know about my shortcomings. I either chose to not be myself around Him, or I distracted myself and never prayed at all. Somehow, I thought this would make God love me more? Uh, yeah . . .

- **LOVE**—I did not love Him as much as I would have people believe. I was deathly afraid of Him even though He is Love. I was so scared to die and meet Him face-to-face. And I did not let Him love me.

- **FORGIVENESS**—I did not allow Him to forgive me. I always thought that my sin was somehow more significant than God's love. And I did not forgive Him for some things. Wow, I can be bold.

- **PEACE**—For a period of my life, I blamed Him when life turned hard. I had the attitude that I was really trying to live a good life and be kind to other people, but things never seemed to go my way. Why would He be mean to me, someone He supposedly loved?

- **LISTEN/RECEIVE**—I did not listen to Him. I spent all my prayer time either reading, listening to music, or talking to God about my concerns. There was no time for Him to say anything to my soul. My prayer life was too loud.

- **CONFIDENCE**—I did not acknowledge He was my friend in public. Somehow, I needed to overcome embarrassment when I put my cross necklace on or put up religious sayings on my desk at work.

- **ABIDE IN**—I did things separately from Him. I wanted to live my life somehow, fix my sins on my own, and show up to God a perfect human being for Him to finally love me as the most awesome person on the planet. I know. Really dumb.

- **SURRENDER**—I was the one putting conditions on unconditional love. I refused to relinquish control to God. I wanted to tell Him when it was okay to forgive me, when he could love me, and when He was trustworthy.

- **FREEDOM**—I did not feel free. I felt overwhelmed, judged, unworthy, enslaved.

And put the book down, here comes the lightning bolt. Hahahahaha. Just kidding. As you can see, I was so far away from what God wanted for me.

I am not sure if you see some of yourself in any of this. It was alarming to me when I realized that I was not living out in my heart what I proclaimed with my mouth and with my life.

Why does all of this matter? What does this get us? God cannot unleash His love and mercy on us if we do not believe Him 100%. Therefore, we cannot work with Him to change the world. I genuinely think that we do not see some of the change in the world because the world is waiting for us to love God and to honestly believe that we are indeed loved by God.

Let's take a closer look at my failings. (Wow, this is super fun to write about and share with the world.)

TRUST—Are you sure, God, you meant what you said? Are you super sure? Really, really sure? Or just kind of sure?

Never be afraid to trust an unknown future to a known God.

—Corrie Ten Boom

I remember one of my theology professors at Notre Dame. He taught a course on grace that kind of blew apart my world and challenged me to wrap my arms around how much God provides grace to us all. The Mother Teresa's of the world receive grace right along with the serial killers (if they repent). Yes, that is true.

One day while we were in class, he made a comment about the cutesy posters sold in the Christian bookstores: "God is Love" or "Trust God" or "Faith is not faith until it is all you are holding onto." This was my favorite quote, though, as I had this poster hanging in my college dorm room. And of course, the cuteness of these sayings on the signs is only surpassed by the kitten or snuggly puppy. Trust God? I am not confident that I trusted my dog a ton when she was a puppy. Very cute, but not quite trustworthy. It was very similar to my teenagers—very cute. Not sure I get the full story all of the time. Lol.

I bet you are wondering where this is going. Trusting God is not easy, and it is not just a cutesy phrase. I fear, however, that many of us, including myself at times, do not trust God. We do not believe what He says though we claim we do. Trust me—you can do that—I have not always trusted God. I do now, but it has taken *a lot* of work to get here.

So, I want you to take a second and read each line in the list below. Take these one-by-one, close your eyes, and spend a few minutes in silence and ask yourself: What if I 100% believed this statement? Not 50%, not 75%, not 99%, but 100%? What would happen if I were all in? How would my life change?

- God loves me unconditionally—There is nothing I can do to make Him love me less or to make Him love me more.

- All of my sins are forgiven by the grace of God.

- I have no reason to fear.

- I am a worthy son or daughter of God.

- Jesus is my friend.

I would surmise that you have read about God in the Bible at some point. (If not, never fear, you can always get started.) God mentions all these assertions throughout the Bible. For example, a version of "do not be afraid" or "fear not" appears over 300 times in the Bible. All of us, myself included, doubt these assertions much of the time. Why? We do not trust God.

And now, I am going to say something that will shock you. Are you ready?

If you do not believe the statements above, wait for it—you are calling God, the Creator of the Universe and the ultimate unconditional lover, *a liar.*

He tells us that He loves us, and we do not believe Him. He tells us that we are forgiven, and we do not believe Him. He asks us to trust Him with our lives, and we are terrified to make that leap. I was. I am right there with everyone else.

When I was in silent prayer, this thought came to me, and I was devastated. I could barely catch my breath. Was this truly what I thought of God? I did not want it to be, so I prayed to Jesus that He would help me change. And then I had just to take the leap of faith and believe God. I had to simply decide to trust God, to believe what He told me, and start living my life as though I believed everything God told us about Him. It gets easier with time, but at the very beginning, I remember it was a challenge to change my thought process and trust that God is indeed who He says He is.

We all need to trust Him. It is the basis of our relationship, and we cannot connect with Him if we hold back part of ourselves because we do not wholeheartedly believe Him.

HONESTY—God can see me when I hide. Seriously, He really can, and He can see you too.

Your gift to God is Honesty. His gift to you is Truth.

—Leonard Jacobson

I remember when I was a kid, I used to get in trouble or get mad at my parents for some reason and then hide. Of course, I thought I was an incredibly sly kid and was sure no one knew about my super-secret hideout in my bedroom closet, where I stewed for hours in the dark before falling asleep. I was sure they were absolutely panicked about not being able to find me. Boy, was I smart! Until one day, when my mom thought I had been taking cover for too long. "Dinnertime!" she announced as she slowly slid the solid wood closet door off to the side, blinding me with daylight. "I know you have been in there for hours. You must be hungry." Crap, I was found out. I had to rethink where I was going to disappear.

Being a tomboy as a little girl, I searched for a place outside my house as a new hideaway. I loved to climb trees, and I had a favorite tree in the backyard. Ah, that would be my new place to get away from it all! So, for the following years, I always went there as a refuge. When I was upset at my parents, sister, friends, school, whatever, that was my place. And no one ever found me there. Well, that is what I thought until I was in my 30s, and my mom made some comments similar to "Yeah, that used to crack me up as I watched you climb the tree from the kitchen window, and you thought you were invisible. I never had the heart to tell you that everyone could see you!" O.M.G.

In almost the same way, I thought I had somehow been successful in hiding from God for most of my life. When I was angry, upset, had sinned, and when I could not stand the pressure anymore, I did one of two things. I avoided praying to God, thinking that, in some bizarre way, if I did not talk with Him, He would not know any of my baggage. Or, on other days, I would pray, but I would not tell Him everything. After all, it was not real if I did not tell him, right?

Okay, so I know you are probably rolling your eyes and thinking I am an idiot, but to be honest, most people tend to do this subconsciously. We do not put ourselves all the way out there to be loved by God because we do not feel as though we are worthy and think, *If He really knew us, He would not still love us.*

We need to put ourselves out there with God fully. He meets us where we are and works with us to heal the pain in our lives, to let go of our unhealthy worldly attachments, and to unleash our goodness for all the world to see.

LOVE—Be afraid, be very afraid. Uh, maybe not.

God's love is based on nothing and, therefore, is the most basic and secure fact in my life.

—Peter Van Breeman SJ

So, we talk a lot about God's love for us. How about our love for God? We are supposed to love Him unconditionally, just as He loves us unconditionally. When I looked at my friendship with God, I started to recognize that I was not wildly in love with Him. I was fiercely scared of who He was. This was not good.

"Should I go to the hospital?" I asked my husband, yet again.

"I think you are having a panic attack, Bert." (Bert is my nickname.)

"Feels like a heart attack. I don't think I can breathe," I responded. It kind of felt like it did before, but I thought it was different enough it warranted an evaluation. Off to the emergency room we went. *Again.* I think this was about the fourth time in as many years. I knew I was going to die. I just knew it. Cold sweat poured over me as we made our way to the ER. I honestly thought I was about to meet my Maker, and I was terrified over my fear of meeting the God who unconditionally loved me.

Yeah, read that again. I was afraid of meeting an all-loving, all-forgiving, all-merciful God. Instead of having a feeling of comfort that on some level, death would bring me to the God who loved me so much, I was horrified I would be rejected because I did not meet some kind of criteria. If I were honest with myself, I was dreadfully afraid of God. It was at this point I started a journey of trying to figure out why in the world I was so petrified of a God who loved me so incredibly much. That thought process is not even logical. To add insult to injury, what kind of healthy relationship has one person incredibly frightened of the other person? I would not have that kind of relationship with a human, so why was I subjecting God to my fear? He had done nothing to deserve that. He never told me that He hated me. I made all of that up due to my insecurities and the decision not to spend time developing a relationship with Him. This was all my fault.

The truth that God loves us unconditionally is comforting and somewhat unbelievable at the same time. Most of us in our lives have that sinking feeling of *if they only knew,* or *if God only knew,* then He would not love me.

Many of the relationships we have in our lives are conditional. At work, we develop friendships with our coworkers and supervisors, and for many of us, those friendships ended when there were layoffs, or we moved to another job. We were liked when we were needed. Some of us are estranged from individual family members, which happens when there is too big a wedge in our relationship. Many people have been abused by others and taken advantage of and disappointed by other people's actions. There are typically very few people, if any, in our lives that love us mostly unconditionally. I am not trying to depress everyone, but our fellow humans are imperfect like we are.

It is sometimes hard to look at God differently and to let go of some of our day-to-day human experiences and genuinely know and trust God whose love eclipses our wildest imaginations. How do we do that? Are you sitting down? I know this is going to sound so incredibly out of left field, but *you just do it*. I hate to say, "fake it until you make it." However, you need to plow through those overwhelming feelings of disbelief and choose to believe even when you do not feel it. No one deserves God. Welcome His love and honor Him by serving Him.

Much has been written about Mother Teresa and her struggles with not feeling God's love. She continued to do His work with the most destitute people under the direst of circumstances. She did not feel His love for most of her life, but she knew He loved her. We can use her inspiration in our lives. Many people talk about love being a choice, not a feeling. Well, believing that God loves you unconditionally is a choice most of the time and not a feeling. Sometimes, you will feel it, but those are few and far between for many people. When you doubt that you are indeed cherished, you need to push that thought out of your head and simply believe.

What does it look like to trust and know that God loves you, unconditionally?

Well, in my experience, I felt like a massive load lifted off of me. I used to carry around this guilt and shame all of the time. And the fear—oh, the fear. Was I good enough? Was I going to heaven? What if I died today? Have I fixed enough of myself to even be in the vicinity of a loving God?

To be quite honest, I was a little bit of a nut job about some of this. It got to the point where I was deathly afraid of dying. I freaked out at every little change in my body. Was my heart beating differently, and why was my leg sore? Was it a blood clot? Why was my eye twitching? (Well, I knew the answer to that one. It was because I was a stress ball.)

Now, I have a lot less of all of this worry and hypochondria. Sure, sometimes at work or when I argue with one of my teens, my eye twitches, but that is another book for another time.

I could drop dead today, and I know I will land in the arms of God. For real. He loves me so much. Correction—He loves me—unconditionally.

FORGIVENESS—I know you created the whole world and all, but how can you forgive me?

> *If I repent now, will God forgive me? No. But if God forgives you, you will repent.*

> —Rabia Basri

When I got out of college, I started my journey to become a professional golfer. I took a job in the Cleveland area as a golf shop attendant, so I could work and also be able to play the course and take advantage of free driving range balls. It was an awesome setup.

There were a few NFL football players from the local team who frequented the country club, and I will never forget the first day I saw a group of them on the driving range practicing. They were trying to annihilate their golf balls and have them soar over 300 yards. Every once in a while, their shots were phenomenal. Most of the time, the shots they hit skidded on the ground. They wanted to hit the ball far through raw power. Golf does not work like that. It is all about technique, form, and rhythm.

In a moment of sheer deviousness and wanting to needle these guys a bit, I got off work and took my bucket of golf balls to the range. I set up on the driving range where they could all see me and proceeded to rhythmically, slowly, and consistently hit my driver a very, very long way. Of course, they got so frustrated and angry when they saw me—a girl—crush the ball compared to their large and tough physiques. So, what did they do? They tried to hit the ball even harder, and their swings got even faster. And of course, their shots did not improve. They gave up and left in a huff. Yes, I think I heard some swearing.

What in the world does this have to do with forgiveness? We need to do something different to be able to repent. We cannot do what we have always done, albeit harder, and get super frustrated and upset that we may as well give up since we cannot change ourselves. Like those professional football players needed to take a step back and ask for some help and change their perspective and swing the club differently, I needed to accept God has forgiven me, and He will be the One to change me through His friendship with me. I spin my wheels if I do the same thing over and over in different ways. Pure willpower on our part does not really work. It is only when we access the God within us that we can change, and the only way to access that part of us is to spend time in silence and prayer. We need to listen to the One who can help us so that He can change our perspective. He is not our ultimate golf pro, but He is our ultimate *life pro*. He changes us in spite of ourselves, and we stop the cycle of insanity.

I guess I am weird in a way—or in many ways—but I am a person who used to run *from* God in adversity. There seems to be a tendency to run *to* God when people's worlds start to fall apart. I used to run away and become angry.

The concept of God's forgiveness and mercy is, in my opinion, one of the most difficult concepts to accept. I know I have struggled with this myself. We try and try to do the best we can and fall miserably short all the time.

As I mentioned earlier, I think that we have been looking at everything backward. We have been working to be better people from our willpower. We tell ourselves that the better, more loving people we are, the closer to God we are and the more spiritual/religious we are. It is up to us and only us to heal our hurts and lessen our pain. We think that then, God will be happier with us, and we will make it to heaven.

The first thing I notice about this approach is that there is no relationship there. I am doing my best, and then I get judged. The second obvious factor here is that we are the broken, fallible people who come with a whole bunch of baggage. (Some we gave ourselves and some that was given to us.) We are the last people who can fix the mess we created, nor can we *try harder* by doing the same thing repeatedly. We need God to heal us. His forgiveness and love allow us to repent and change. We cannot earn it. We don't deserve it. But we need to accept it. It is our responsibility to accept this gift we did not earn or deserve because rejecting the gift ruins our lives and ruins others' lives in the world. Those others cannot experience God's love because we are choosing to wallow in our own angst.

God loves and forgives us, and then we change. We do not change and then have God love and forgive us. Mercy and love create the environment for one's heart to be softened and to understand that their pain *can* indeed be lifted away. Being loved in our imperfection allows us to stop stressing out and feeling overwhelmed at our failures. We can know we are loved as we are and let God's love come in and heal us. We are in a relationship with him.

Many of our churches preach that if we do "xyz" then God will give us "abc." If we give money until it hurts, we will be rewarded. If we live a good life, we will be blessed with great relationships and wealth. This is a bunch of &*($#& (uh . . . stuff 😊). You can look around and see this does not happen. Spend some time looking beyond the developed world, and you can see the two-thirds of the people in the world who are in poverty. These formulas do not work for them at all. I worked for a nonprofit that focused on eliminating modern-day slavery around the world. You cannot tell me that little kids sold into sexual slavery by their parents did something terribly wrong, and therefore, God will never bless them. Many of these kids end up dead in ditches before the age of 12. Did they not live good enough lives to be blessed by God? Hardly.

Remember the earlier reference to *The Matrix?* There is no spoon. There is no formula for all of this. Let God do the heavy lifting for you. But you are responsible for showing up. You have to develop your relationship with Him to understand His love and mercy and to find your peace.

PEACE—Why can't You fix everything, God? I gave you the list! I must need a new agent . . .

May the peace of God disturb you always.

—Anthony DeMello

The peace of God is out there. It really is. I missed it for the majority of my life—until now. I had to change my view of the world and God to find it.

I had been a softball player for most of my life. When I did not make the Little League All-Star team after being on the team for a few years, I was done with rather subjective team sports. Of course, most every kid probably thinks that they were slighted at some point in their sports careers. However, for some reason, this event was the last straw for me. I decided to drop softball, volleyball, and basketball. By the way, it was definitely the right call on the basketball; I am short. I decided to pursue golf even though I thought it was an old man's sport. I was in control, and I posted a score. There were no nuances, no politics, and no excuses, only a better or worse score than my competitors. I practiced and practiced until I was able to be competitive.

The first year I went out for the high school team, I shot around 45 per nine holes—this is kind of bad for all non-golfers out there. The team was all guys except for me, and I had to play from their tees. The next summer, I spent all my days on the golf course, trying desperately to catch up to the skill level of everyone around me. When it was time to try out that fall, I not only made the team but was one of the top players. It was something I could do that I thoroughly enjoyed. The dream to be a professional golfer was planted.

I could see myself like the guy from *Chariots of Fire*.[9] This is an old movie for those of you born after 1975. It won the Academy Award for Best Picture in 1982. It is about two runners—one Christian and one Jewish—and their quest for getting into the Olympics. Eric Liddell was the Christian, and there is a point in the movie in which he gives a speech on the beach after a race to a small crowd of people. He offered them the wisdom that faith is similar to running a race. It is challenging, and there are many highs and lows. The only way to get through this life is to find the power within you. If you seek Christ and commit to love, only then can you run a straight race.

---

9   Hugh Hudson, *Chariots of Fire* (1981; London: Enigma Productions, 1997), DVD.

I could always see myself utilizing my athletic notoriety as a platform for ministry. It was a win/win for God and me, right? And then, wham! The dream ended.

I had started my career as a semi-professional golfer, but my back had been giving me a lot of trouble. One day, I leaned over to get the TV remote off the floor in my apartment, and the most excruciating pain shot through my back. I went face down on the living room floor. And seriously, I stayed there for hours, unable to even crawl. I yelled to my husband, "I have fallen, and I can't get up!" I can still see the woman yelling this on the floor in the LifeAlert TV commercial, and though I was in agonizing pain, I started to laugh. Falling is not a funny thing, but I laughed through my tears. It was bound to be a massive uphill battle to be able to play golf again.

I went to the chiropractor a day later, and he took x-rays. He told me that my back looked like an 80-year-old who had been in a car accident. The top of my spine was twisted one way. The bottom was curved another way, and there was a kink in the middle of my back where I had ripped a rib or two off my vertebrae. It was all from practicing so hard to reach my dreams. I went to that chiropractor for adjustments multiple times a day for months because my back simply would not hold the adjustments.

I tried to continue playing a few months after chiropractic treatments and physical therapy. The pain was simply too great. I had to face reality; I would be struggling with a ton of pain for the rest of my life if I chose to continue to compete. As it is, I had a lot of back pain over the years, even when I did not play golf, so at the age of 26 years old, I hung up the clubs. And boy, was I mad.

I worked so hard and gave up so much of my time and was utterly devoted to being a successful golfer. I thought God put it on my heart to pursue this as a career, and I could use it to touch people's lives. *This is a bunch of crap!* Why didn't God show up when I did what I thought He wanted? I know this was a total first-world issue and it is doubtful anyone would be disappointed I was unable to be a professional golfer, but it was my dream. Golf was my way to serve God, truly believing it was what I was supposed to do. He even blessed me with the talent to make it if I had not had such an issue with my back. *WTH, God?*

As one could expect, I had a severe identity crisis after that. I also started having other pain issues and sickness and depression. My marriage was unraveling on top of all of this. The peace of Christ? Nope, not here. Not one ounce of peace was anywhere to be found. I was ready to chuck this whole thing. This sounds so stupid to write down and share in a book, but I think the disappointments in our lives have the potential of sending our spiritual lives into a tailspin. Where was God? I did the *right* things, so where was He? Isn't it all supposed to work out?

As you can tell from my spiral into the black hole, the concept of Christ's peace had been elusive to me. I knew God's love was supposed to provide peace, but it did not for me, to be honest. This was my fault. Why in the world was I pinning life circumstances and events to God's love? As a pastor once said in a homily I heard 20 plus years ago, "God is not your agent." He does not go around making our lives easy and answering all of the demands we request.

To find God's peace, we need to completely detach the events in our lives and our expectations of God from His love for us. These are two separate things. If they were not independent,

> To find God's peace, we need to completely detach the events in our lives and our expectations of God from His love for us.

much of our life and our relationships with God and our peace would be out of our control. We are in control of the level of peace we allow into our lives. It is up to us. I chose for a long time to have almost no peace. Unfortunately, I had to look into the mirror and understand that I decided that. Me—I did that.

God's peace is constant in my life now. Why? I know that no event, no disappointment, no person, no failure, no sin, and no tragedy can separate me from God. He is in this with me. He knows that the world is imperfect and that we are all imperfect and loves us anyway. We need to know that God is by our side during all the chaos in our lives. He is not separate from us, and He does not use puppet strings to make our lives bad if He hates us for something, nor does He make things good if we are somehow chosen. He loves us all and wants us to feel this peace and love throughout our lives, no matter what happens. We can love others and glorify God no matter what our life circumstances. We need to let go of our own selfish ways and again, simply let God love us and help us throughout our lives. Helen Keller once eloquently stated, "I do not want the peace that passeth understanding. I want the understanding which bringeth peace."

LISTEN/RECEIVE—Blah, Blah, Blah: I am sorry, God, but did you say something? Blah, Blah, Blah.

God speaks in the silence of the heart. Listening is the beginning of prayer.

—Mother Teresa

I was at Mass one Saturday morning at Holy Trinity Parish in Georgetown. It was a 7:30 a.m. Mass, and I was all excited to go, relax, pray, and start my weekend on a positive note. As I walked into the chapel after dipping my hand in the holy water and performing the sign of the cross, I sat down and prayed. No one else was in the chapel, but I was early. The silence was simply serene.

As 7:30 a.m. approached, one other gentleman came into the chapel, and then Mass started. I forgot to pick up a book from the back and panicked as it became evident that when the priest said something, it was only this other guy and me who were there to respond. As a theology major who grew up going to church every weekend of her life and then some, this should not have been an uncomfortable situation, except that it was. When you are in a big group, you just say the words that everyone else is saying. It is like the difference between singing a song along with the radio vs. singing it without any assistance. Wow, it became apparent that, after all these years, I was not really paying attention to what I was saying anymore. It became ritualistic and was way too familiar.

One of the most significant transitions in prayer comes from the recitation of prayers, asking God for things, and offering gratitude to listening in silence. There is nothing wrong with the various ways of praying. However, we seem to have lost the art of being quiet, and this is where we profoundly experience God. This is where we provide space and time for Him to speak to us in the silence. We can cut through the noise and the chaos of every day and hear God in our souls—our true selves. So much of our days are attached to our jobs, families, sin, egos, addictions, etc., that we cannot hear ourselves think. In fact, we start to lose sight of who we really are.

It is in the silence that we not only find God, but we find our true selves. Is that not what a relationship is all about? Taking time to listen to another person allows us to know them more, and it also allows them to reflect and delve into our lives. In the silence of our relationship with God, we get to know Him more fully and allow Him to connect into our lives. In return, He gets to know us more, and we can connect into His presence and His plan to spread His love to all the world. It is a give and take just like the relationships we have with others.

So, as I started to learn to be silent, I realized I had not really been listening to God all these years. I was trying to have a relationship with the Creator of the Universe, and I never showed up. I often repeated routine prayers, said what I needed, and reflected on my day, but I never gave God the space to show up in my life. It cannot work that way. It is our responsibility to show up and face the silence. We need to face ourselves and trust that God is there in the stillness with us. This is such an important concept that I devoted Chapter 6 to the idea of learning how to listen to God.

CONFIDENCE—Is my cross necklace small enough?

I hope for the day when everyone can speak again of God without embarrassment.

—Paul Tillich

I bought a crucifix from a jeweler in Texas in my early 20s. (A crucifix is a cross with Jesus on it and represents Christ's death on the cross.) I wore it all of the time when I was golfing. Again, I was trying to be like the *Chariots of Fire* person. The necklace reminded me of who I am at the core. Every time I put it on and caught a glimpse of myself in a mirror, I remembered what was truly important. Nothing else is as important as my faith. Nothing.

When I lost the ability to play golf, I worked in various jobs. While not having an official policy preventing the display of religious symbols, many of them seemed to have a culture of not wanting to deal with people who were proud of their faith. And as I have learned over the years, many times, people of faith are despised by society's mainstream atheistic trends.

So, I ended up taking my reminders down in my cubicle. My crosses around my neck got smaller. Or I chose more abstract symbols so I would know what they meant, but no one else would know. I did not want to deal with the looks and the rolling eyes anymore.

Like most things in this book that are my failures in life, this is embarrassing to admit. I love God so much, and He is my best friend, and I have been self-conscious and ashamed at admitting to his friendship at certain times.

Another massive strike against me for the friend-of-the-year award with God.

I wanted Him to be proud of me and be by my side, and I was mortified to show God the same courtesy. My priorities were askew, and I needed to decide to be confident in my relationship with God. When I am confident in Him, He can work through me. I need to feel confident that Jesus lives in me. Actually, when I play down my relationship with God, I am also concealing my true self. I cannot let Him work through me because I deny that He is even real. Hmmm, I think there was an example of this in the Scriptures. Let's see. Who denied Jesus publicly in the Bible? Peter denied Jesus three times and was scared because the world was against Jesus, and he was associated with Him. There always has been worldly pressure to hide our relationships with God. We need not to care what people think anymore.

ABIDE IN—Can you come over Jesus, and we can stare at our cell phones together?

As the branch cannot bear fruit by itself, unless it abides in the vine, neither can you, unless you abide in me.

—John 15:4

My son was dying for a sleepover with one of his friends. As a mom of three boys, overnights always cause a fair amount of trepidation. I am always trying to figure out ahead of time what is going to break, what will be ruined, who will get upset, etc. So much fun. Every time. However, it is good for the kids to get together with their friends. I do love to see my kids' joy when they have a fun night with friends, even when there is an aftermath to deal with.

I woke up in the middle of the night and saw my kids in the living room. They had the 55" TV in the living room and then brought up the smaller TV from downstairs and set it up. As I passed them when I went to the kitchen to get some water, I noticed they were both playing video games but not the same games. So, they were not playing together. And they were on their phones, texting other people.

My big question was, why in the world was this other kid over at my house? There was no interaction between my son and his friend. They were not even playing the same game online!

I feel like this was a picture of me most of my life with my friendship with God. I was always in the same room with Him but was not abiding in Him. I was not letting Him dwell in me. I was right there with Him, but doing my own thing. We were not doing anything together. Why? It was as if He was sitting on the couch next to me, waiting for me to see Him. Meanwhile, I was busy trying to get myself together so I would not be judged. I was living my life separate and expecting that I would somehow be close.

Like my kids needed to either turn the games off, engage in a conversation or game together, or at least play the same game online, I needed to decide to live my life with God and invite Him into my day-to-day.

What was preventing me from doing this? Fear. It all goes back to believing God loves me unconditionally and forgives me for everything. You cannot abide in Him and be with

Him by your side every day if you do not believe He accepts you 100% as you are right now. This is why this is the first thing we need to do is to understand and trust and accept. Nothing works with a relationship if we do not trust God first. Nothing.

SURRENDER—You can only love me if I let you.

Don't get upset with your imperfections. Surrender to the Power of God's Love, which is greater than our weaknesses.

—Saint Francis de Sales

We can be total control freaks. We want a feeling that everything is in our influence, and we run away from anything that makes us feel as though we are losing control. It is one thing to control our lives, but it is a whole other level of crazy to think we can control God.

What, you say? We can never control God. And yet, we all try to. Don't believe He loves you? Don't let Him forgive you? Don't forgive yourself when He has already forgiven you? Yep. We are all trying to control God's level of love and forgiveness for us. God is Love—nothing else. He cannot do anything but love us unconditionally because that is who He is.

In my experience, I have tried to redefine who God says He is into a conditional loving God who does not fully forgive. I wanted to try and control how He interacted with me. Throughout my life, I have chosen to deny His love for me and to reel in my self-pity because I would not surrender to God and let go of my control and limits on Him.

Peter, as I mentioned at the beginning of the book, surrendered to God. He made a ton of mistakes, but He ran to Jesus when He first saw Him. Peter knew that Peter was

Peter, and God was God. Jesus was exactly who He said He was. He was the Good News, offering the ultimate love and absolute forgiveness.

When we choose to run away from God instead of running toward Him, we look to control Him and limit and regulate His interactions with us. Peter did this, too, and Jesus went from calling Peter the Rock of the Church in one verse and a few short verses later, referred to him as Satan, literally. Peter tried to tell Jesus how everything should work out, what Jesus foretold and tried to limit Him, and Jesus called him out on it. *"He said all this quite openly. And Peter took him aside and began to rebuke him. But turning and looking at his disciples, he rebuked Peter and said, 'Get behind me, Satan! For you are setting your mind not on divine things but on human things'"* (Mark 8:32-33*)*. If Peter were not on the same page as Jesus and tried to control everything, he would be a hindrance. Just like when we try to control God, we become a hindrance to what He is attempting to accomplish through us.

We need to be comfortable losing control and letting Him love and forgive us, and in the end, when we do as He says, we can love and forgive ourselves as well. If God can forgive us, do we think we are more powerful and can impede that forgiveness?

FREEDOM—God, is this the key to get out of prison, and I have had it all along?

Freedom from all attachment is the realization of God as Truth.

—Mahatma Gandhi

As I alluded to before, when we brought our sons home from Russia, they had a hard time letting go of things like food, toys, and habits. They did not have the freedom to understand that they were in a loving place and that no one would steal their food or their toys.

I feel as though I spent a lot of my years of building (or not really building) my friendship with God, like my kids played with their toys. How could I keep the unhealthy attachments in my life and still want God? It is impossible to stay in control of one's life and fully reach for God at the same time. So, I had one life in one hand and the new life that God was offering, on the other hand. With both hands being so full, I could not really do anything.

It was kind of like starting a healthy diet but hiding the chocolate bars in the cupboard, drawer, or backpack. (Well, that is at least what I hear people do. 😊) My kids had stuffed their mouths almost to the point of choking. In the end, their fear of not having food—which drove that behavior—could have killed them. Again, they could not do anything with all the food in their mouths. Some of it would have to come out if they were to swallow any of the food.

When we come from a sense of lack and a sense that we don't want to let go of things in our lives that are hurting us (our old "toys"), we are stuck, in pain, and panic. We can never rest in God and feel free until we let go of our old thinking and realize that we come from abundance. There is nothing in the world that can take the peace of God away from us. We do not need anything other than to know God is the only Truth, so there is really nothing that we can attach to in this life that will provide us with the peace, nor the pleasure of knowing God. When we fully understand that, we are free. Nothing can touch us but the love of God.

God loves you period. There is no comma.

So, as one can clearly see, my honest assessment of my relationship with God led me to a plethora of painful truths about myself. It was scary on the one

God loves you period.
There is no comma.

hand, but very freeing in other ways. All of my cards were on the table with God. I was spiritually vulnerable for the first time. No walls. No excuses. No running. Just me and my failures before my friend, Jesus. I never felt so completely and utterly loved and free in my entire life.

Part 2

BEING GOD AWE-FULL—LETTING GOD HEAL YOU

··· 4 ···

The Perfect Imperfect Friendship with God— Delivering a Very Different Type of Friend with Benefits

We cannot experience from God that which we refuse to believe.

—Impact Ministries

TO BE GOD Awe-full, we must lean on Him. We have to let go of ourselves and watch the Awe-fullness happen.

As the bus approached a road in the middle of the woods, I was unsure what to expect. The bus parked in the lot as the rain drizzled outside. I wondered if there could be colder, damper day to do all of this. Ugh. We grabbed our belongings, got off the bus, and headed into the woods with our teams. Yep, this was corporate team building at its best. We were somewhere south of San Francisco, isolated from the rest of the world, and it was time to bond.

My team went from activity to activity, working together to overcome all kinds of obstacles, feeling very accomplished when we succeeded, and very frustrated at our failures. All-in-all, we did pretty well and did not break out in too many fights. I distinctly remember two of the activity stations because I struggled with them.

One of our activities was to stand on a tree stump about three to four feet off the ground and fall backward into our teammates' arms. Of course, when it was my turn, they upped the ante. I stood on the stump with my back facing them while another person laid on the ground behind me, and everyone had their hands at their sides until I started to fall. Someone signaled the team to put their hands up and catch me. When they caught me, it prevented me from getting hurt and stopped me from killing the person on the ground.

So, as my luck had it, they chose the woman with the faintest voice to be the person to tell everyone I was starting to fall. I leaned back and began to fall, but I heard nothing. *Absolutely nothing.* There was no signal for people to catch me. I am not sure some people were even paying attention. Then, I heard, "Oh, my God!" from the crowd, and thank God, people sprang into action and caught me rather low to the ground and right on top of my coworker. Tragedy averted.

Another activity on that outing that brings me heartburn when I think of it was when I decided to be one of the people who climbed a 60-foot tree then had to walk out on a plank and jump off. Our guide belayed below me, but it would be a free-fall until she caught me. I am afraid of heights. I thought I would face my fears and do this exercise, but I never knew the intensity of the fears I had. For some reason, our guide had the group sing "Happy Birthday" to get me to jump off the tree. I guess there is some psychological reason that particular song is supposed to make people feel comfortable enough to take a chance. Well, I could jump or climb down the rickety ladder on the tree back to safety. I chose to jump. And I lived—I am writing this book here some 20 plus years later.

What in the world does this have to do with the chapter on having God heal me? I have to trust Him first and know He is there through the good and the bad, through the *almost* tragedies, and through the *real* tragedies. You have to figuratively jump out of the tree and trust that He is going to belay you. God is always is going to catch you.

I think most people have the mental experience of my first team building nightmare-creating exercise. We feel as though we are going to blindly trust God, lean back into Him, slam into the ground, and hurt ourselves and possibly maim others around us.

So, what do we do instead? We stand there on the stump and never fall back. What happens if we do that? We never thoroughly learn to trust God and cannot live His dream for us, which is actually the deep desire that we have in our hearts. Even though it was frightfully scary to lean back and not hear a sound, you know what—the team caught me. It was definitely not how I envisioned it at all or as smooth as I would have liked it to have been, but I learned that this group of people really had my back (literally and figuratively—lol). So, the next time I would be more confident when I needed to trust them. I knew they would be there for me.

I noted if I were really going to trust in God, I needed to have enough faith to lean back and fall because the more I did this, the more that I would trust God. And the more confidence I would have in Him in the future. Proverbs 3:5-6, states, *"Trust in the Lord with all your heart, and do not rely on your own insight. In all your ways acknowledge him, and he will make straight your paths."*

This is where all of the magic begins in our relationship with God.

Once we can trust Him, believe in Him that He is who He says He is, and understand that we are immensely loved, He can heal us and use us for His good. Without our ability to see this, we are dead in the water, merely going through the motions and not impacting the world as we should.

Ah, shucks, I cannot change the world. That is ridiculous. Who am I? Blah, blah, blah, blah . . . I knew you were going to think that, so I took care of writing out your thoughts.

You know what? Jesus needed friends, or you and I would not be talking about Him today. Seriously. While I was writing this book, it really struck me that Jesus needed friends. The Savior of the World, King of Kings, Wonderful Counselor, and the Son of God needed friends. He still needs them, and He is calling all of us to be His friends. John 15:15 states, *"I do not call you servants any longer, because the servant does not know what the master is doing; but I have called you friends, because I have made known to you everything that I have heard from my Father."* Not only did He need His friends' support, but He needed them to understand God's love so much it would change them, and they could go out and tell the world about Him. Hmmm, I read about this somewhere before.

I always thought that Jesus' need for close friends was over 2,000 years ago. And honestly, I read the Bible with the lens that all of these people needed Jesus and not vice versa. They did need Him, but He also needed them.

Let's take a quick look at how some of these friends supported Jesus.

Friends of Our Savior

John the Baptist

Jesus needed someone to baptize Him to fulfill the Scriptures. John the Baptist really thought this was unnecessary because he was an imperfect person baptizing God's Son. However, John fulfilled his responsibility in the history of salvation and baptized Jesus in Mark 1:9.

Mary Magdalene

Mary Magdalene always gets such a bad wrap. Depending on what you read, she was either a prostitute or an amazing disciple to Jesus—or both.

What did her friendship with our Lord do for Him? Mary was a trusted friend whom He could rely on and stood by Him through thick and thin. She spread His joy and took care of Him. She and the other Mary were the first people at the tomb, saw that He was resurrected, and ran to tell everyone else. *"After the sabbath, as the first day of the week was dawning, Mary Magdalene and the other Mary went to see the tomb"* (Matthew 28:1). Mary believed what Jesus told everyone before He died and rejoiced in the fact that He rose even when people did not believe her. He knew He could trust her, and she was a great disciple.

John, The Beloved Disciple

John the Apostle was referred to as the Beloved Disciple (John 13:23). He, Peter, and James witnessed the Transfiguration. Jesus sent John and Peter to prepare for the Last Supper, and during the Last Supper, John sat next to Jesus. When Jesus was alive, John was instrumental in Jesus' ministry. He was also extremely foundational to His ministry after the Resurrection. Mary Magdalene first told Peter and John about the empty tomb, and they ran to see it for themselves and spread the news to others.

One of the most touching scenes in the New Testament is where Jesus is dying on the cross and tells John to take care of His mother and family. Jesus was worried about the care of His family and needed others to help Him take care of them after His death.

Stop for a second and think about that. Jesus needed His friend to take care of His family. We are all His friends, and He needs us to take care of His family—everyone—after His death and Resurrection.

In Acts, there are many more accounts of John spreading the Good News. He even ended up getting thrown into prison with Peter (Acts 4:3). Nothing could stop these disciples from spreading the love of God to all.

Peter

Ahh, Peter. I love this guy.

Peter was there to lead the church. His relationship with Jesus gave Him the tools and wherewithal to guide the people in the new community that was forming.

So, Jesus needed Peter for his leadership skills, but He also needed Peter for his boat. You see, Jesus preached to the multitudes many times in Peter's boat. Yes, Jesus borrowed His friend's boat to preach the Good News.

Even though Peter failed immensely at times, he was the one who was written about the most in the Gospels as taking action. He tried to walk on water and failed. He pushed back on Jesus when He wanted to wash Peter's feet, but then Peter agreed to it when Jesus said, *"Unless I wash you, you have no share with me.' Simon Peter said to him, 'Lord, not my feet only but also my hands and my head!'"* (John 13:8-9). When Jesus was arrested, some attribute Peter as the one who cut off the soldier's ear. Peter was in the trenches, continually trying to figure out His faith and live it. He so desperately wanted to be Jesus' friend, and although he failed a lot, he also succeeded more than others.

One of the hardest accounts to read of Peter in the Bible is his denial of Jesus three times. When I read these passages, I always cringe because I wonder if I would be able to be courageous enough to admit to knowing Jesus in those circumstances. Even then, though, when Jesus was resurrected,

He gave Peter a chance to repent by asking him if he loved
Him and would feed His sheep. Jesus asked this three times
to coincide with each denial (John 21:15-17).

Jesus gave Peter a job to do. Peter was imperfect, but the
more He knew Jesus and witnessed His Resurrection, the
more Peter understood the Good News and, in turn, became
less afraid. He moved from being frightened and denying
Jesus to knowing his mission of spreading God's love to the
point of imprisonment and, ultimately, death.

Did Jesus need Peter's friendship? Absolutely. Where
would we be without Peter's willingness to be a friend to
Jesus? Our Christian history would probably look much different. I am sure God would have found a way, but Peter's
"yes" did so much to spread the Good News.

As an aside, notice that Peter's life as a doubter and denier
was much more stressful and fearful than when he trusted
God and understood the Good News from his time with the
Resurrected Christ. He was free when his relationship with
Jesus was everything, free even when he was imprisoned and
eventually killed for spreading the Gospel.

Other Friends of Our God

How about some examples from the Hebrew Bible where
ridiculously imperfect people were the perfect friends to God?

Moses

Moses loved God but wanted nothing to do with leading
people out of Egypt. Even though God spoke to him via a
burning bush, Moses still thought he was not equipped for
the task. He was not a good speaker and knew in his heart
that he had killed a man. *"But Moses said to the Lord, "O my
Lord, I have never been eloquent, neither in the past nor even
now that you have spoken to your servant; but I am slow of speech
and slow of tongue." The Lord said to him, "Who gives speech to*

73

mortals? Who makes them mute or deaf, seeing or blind? Is it not I, the Lord? Now go, and I will be your mouth and teach you what you are to speak" (Exodus 4:10-12). After further resistance, Moses did finally say, "yes." And God, of course, had a significant plan for Moses. Even though Moses fought God all the way, God was able to take his reluctant "yes" and free the Israelites.

David

David embodies some of the best and the worst in all of us. Lust? Yep. Murderer? Yep. On the other hand, he was a great leader and warrior and an incredible musician. Even in sin, he persevered in his relationship with his God. David wrote many of the Pslams that showed him praising God, crying out to God, repenting, etc. He maintained his connection to God even through his most sinful and dark times. I love Psalm 40:1-3: *"I waited patiently for the Lord; he inclined to me and heard my cry. He drew me up from the desolate pit, out of the miry bog, and set my feet upon a rock, making my steps secure. He put a new song in my mouth, a song of praise to our God. Many will see and fear, and put their trust in the Lord."* U2 has a beautiful song about this Psalm, simply called "40."

What this all did for David, though, was allow him to overlook others' sin and see the good and evil in others, as God did with him. The Psalms provide such a rich spiritual resource in the Bible. What if David did not show up for God? What if he had believed God did not love him? What if we did not have the Psalms?

Me

So, I have written extensively here so far how imperfect I am and do not need to rehash all of that. However, I am totally in love with a God who is totally in love with me. I have failed myself, my friends, my enemies, my kids, and my coworkers. But I have also helped these same people. And honestly, I need to remember that sometimes. It is like taking a picture of the one bad branch of a beautiful and healthy apple tree and posting that bad apple picture on social media. People would look at the misleading picture and assume that the whole tree is fruitless or defective when, in fact, it is just that branch. So it is in our lives. Many of us tend to hyper-focus on the list of faults instead of looking at the list of awesomeness that we also have. I know I fall into that trap some-

> We look up and see the dark clouds cover the entire sky when it is, in reality, a bright, sunny day with a few passing clouds.

times. We look up and see the dark clouds cover the entire sky when it is, in reality, a bright, sunny day with a few passing clouds.

But Jesus needs me. He knows that my good (and the good inside most people) outweighs the bad. He can love us, forgive us, teach us, and use our strengths. Just look at the shortlist of Jesus' friends I have referred to. Even though they were imperfect, He knew of the goodness inside them and continued to walk by their side. I think most logical people can look at their lives and see how much their spirituality grew over the time they were in a relationship with Jesus.

You

How about you? Are you willing to let God work on your imperfections as you focus on being friends with Him and emphasizing your strengths? God needs you. He really does. He needs all of us.

So what are some of the benefits that God gets from us being besties with Him?:

- **Deepens His Relationship with Us**—By spending time with Him, He can form a deeper bond with us and a more genuine relationship—one not filled with lies, running away, and dishonesty.

- **Spreads His Love and Joy**—We can absorb more of His unconditional love, and in turn, we can share His love and joy with the world.

- **Forgives His People**—He can show us how to forgive through our experiences with His forgiveness.

- **Touches Our Soul**—He becomes our #1, and we notice Him more. God becomes the basis for everything in our lives. We do not get sidetracked and distracted by worldly things. We can stay focused on what He needs us to do in the world.

- **Brings Stability to His Flock**—We become more stable and self-sufficient because we look for our strength from Him, not from others in this world. When we are emotionally stable, He can better use our abilities. By not spiraling into negativity, we can stay more positive for ourselves, our families, our friends, our coworkers, and the world.

- **Changes the World**—He can change more of the world because his disciples are more in tune with Him.

- **Allows Him to Be Himself**—We let Him love, forgive, and support us, which is who He is. We allow God to be Himself, not who we box Him up to be. We take Him at His Word.

- **Communicates with Us through Others**—We can hear what He wants us to tell other people. I have had other people tell me God told them to tell me something. Every time, it was something that I needed to hear at that moment. I am so glad that these people listened to God.

- **Bestows Freedom on Us**—His people have freedom from evil, from what others think, from sin, from stress, etc.

- **Cultivates Community**—He allows us to take care of Jesus' family and feel like a community.

- **Nurtures Leaders**—He has fishers of men (people) and has more leaders, prophets, and teachers of His Good News.

- **Forms an Emotional Bond with Us**—We will know Him with our hearts and not in our heads. When we encounter the love and forgiveness of God, nothing else matters. We shout it from the rooftops (ex. Samaritan woman).

- **Encourages More Believers**—He works in us to ensure we genuinely believe the message of Jesus Christ. No more doubts and no one foot on the brake while the other is on the gas. We can accomplish *His* mission.

So, God gets a lot out of us being best friends with Him. He can show Himself to the world through us. That is very cool.

I also thought about what happens when we shut other people, including God, out of our lives. I do not think about what it does to me but what it does to them. There was a time in my life when tons of things were going wrong, yet I chose not to tell anyone for fear of judgment. I was so bottled up with all kinds of emotions and no outlet. So, I began to think about my inability to share with my spouse and friends and what it was doing to *them*. What was my hiding doing to those whom I loved?

I came up with a lot:

- They did not know what was going on, so they did not understand (probably) how I was acting.

- I denied them the opportunity to support and love me.

- I showed that I did not trust them.

- I did not spend moments with them.

- I lied to them, telling them that everything was okay when it was not.

- I drove a wedge into our relationship that was not there before. I actually distanced myself from them and created a gap.

- I missed out on forgiveness.

- I missed out on healing, mercy, love, and grace.

- I missed out on advice.

- I spiraled down into negativity.

- I assumed that no one wanted to deal with me and that re-enforced the notion that I was unworthy.

- I did not experience freedom. I was a slave to my emotions that I could not process on my own.

Every time I did this or sometimes still do this, I drive a deeper wedge between me and my friend or spouse.

Same for God. If I am not there for God and am not a good friend to *Him*, I cannot build that relationship. He comes to *me* with everything—love, mercy, grace, forgiveness, and advice. If I do not let Him in, I get none of these.

In sum, if I am not honest with God and do not spend time with Him, we both lose. We need to stop thinking we are the only people who suffer if we do not develop our relationship with God. God suffers as well, and we limit His ability to work in the world.

Think about that for a minute or two. If we do not trust God, allow Him in our lives, and develop a relationship with Him, we limit His impact in the world. We do not want to do that! "So, yeah, like sorry about that, God. I wanted to do more in the world, but I just could not get myself to believe you." Yikes!

When I lived in Orlando, Florida, there was a very insightful leader in our young adults' group. I will never forget the day when he challenged us, "If we really and truly believe the Good News, then why are we not shouting it from every street corner?" Bam! Mic drop. I thought about that for a while and had to admit that it was because I did not really believe it. When you fully embrace Jesus' unconditional love, you will let others know. You cannot help yourself because you experienced it for yourself and understand the magnitude. The last thing you want is anyone telling you what it is supposed to be like. You know because you have felt it with your heart.

Yes, it is amazing to think that the Creator of the Universe needs us. He does, and we need to stop wallowing around in our self-pity, know that He forgives us and loves us, and go out in the world and let everyone know. That is our job. We are not supposed to be wallflowers and wallowers.

And we are not supposed to hide. The world is waiting for us to love God. The world needs to know we are Jesus' friends. We also need to speak up for Him. Many people in the world have lost their compassion. We need to help people get that back. What we accept now as the treatment of other people is outrageous. Pope Francis was right in the documentary, *Pope Francis: A Man of His Word*, when he mentioned we have lost the ability to face and try to

> The world is waiting for us to love God.

heal other people's suffering.[10] This is the core of Christianity, to be able to address others' pain and have empathy.

But we need to be strong and speak up. There was a video a few years ago about the red cup controversy at Starbucks. The Christmas cups came out that year, and they were plain red. There was no mention of Christmas at all, and many Christians were offended. However, Father Rob Ketcham, the pastor of Christ the King Church in Commack, New York, asked a few simple questions in "The Red Cups of Starbucks" video that he made on *petersboat.net:* Is our Christianity implicit or explicit? Are we the simple red cup that does not say a whole lot? Are our lives focused on what we are for or what we are against? So, the cup controversy was not solely about Starbucks being overt about showing Christmas. We can also look to use it to reflect on our lives and whether we live the Christmas message openly. Fr. Rob reflects, "So, if we are like the light of the world and we come into the darkness and we get mad at the darkness, well then we derive no strength from that and people are left unchanged." We have to know that the world is in darkness, and we need to show love and not be angry over how the world is.

And, my brothers and sisters, this is what is wrong with Christianity today. We should not be focusing on what to curse. We should be focusing on what we are for—God's love. Christ did not continually point out what He was against, but instead, He showed unconditional love. This is what God wants us to spread. People will remain unchanged if we simply get angry with them.

Our friendship with God needs to trust that God will change the people we love. We do not change them by telling them they are wrong all the time. Love them where they are, and God will open up their hearts. Only love opens people's

---

10   Wim Wenders, *Pope Francis: A Man of His Word (2017*; Universal City, CA: Universal Pictures Home Entertainment, 2018), DVD.

hearts. We need to be patient and know that God is working on people's souls in His time. We just need to love. Somewhere along the line, we lost the trust that our God changes people and we do not need to! We don't. He is working on all of our hearts as we speak. When we love people, they change, by God. ☺ Let God be God.

We need to be God's best friends and love people unconditionally, which has the power to open their hearts to be receptive to God working in them. "You know the world is waiting for us to love God. In the meantime, to get mad at the world, you know, for being itself, I think would be a distraction." —Father Rob Ketcham

··· 5 ···

His Love Will Change You— You Don't Change You

There is no fear in love. But perfect love drives out fear.

—1 John 4:18

AWWW . . . THIS used to be kind of a feel-good, cutesy verse in the Bible for me. I made sure that this reading was part of my wedding ceremony. Perfect love drives out fear. So sweet. I think many of us overlook the power in that verse. I know I did for a very long time.

"So, whatcha doing on October 1st?" My husband asked me after I came home from a particularly exhausting day at work. I had no idea where he was going with that question.

"How about we go to Russia and meet our kids?"

"Wha?" was all that I could muster. I remember almost fainting when a tidal wave of emotions hit me at the same time—surprise, shock, fear, joy, trepidation, anxiety, love, and panic. You name it, I felt it. After over a year of filling out all kinds of paperwork, getting the fire chief to inspect our house, having a social worker over many times for the home study, reading books, getting documents apostilled (did not know this was even a thing), and every other imaginary hoop you could think of, we had a call to go to Russia to meet our kids. The call actually came sooner than we thought because the last of the paperwork had only been filed a week or so before the surprise from Jim. Most people wait months, sometimes years.

I think we got the call quickly because we said we would take two or three kids, five years and under, and we did not care if they were boys or girls. Any kid over one had a very difficult time getting adopted in general, and no one really ever wants to take on raising a sibling group. I remember when we told people we were going to take on more than one kid. "You are a saint!" many people said. I used to feel so awesome when people would tell me that, and then one day, it hit me: This was code for saying we were crazy.

So, within the next two weeks, Jim and I got our expedited Russian visas and flew to Russia. We did not know whether we had two or three kids, what ages they were, and if they were boys or girls. No pictures. Nothing. They just told us we had kids that "met our criteria."

We landed at the Moscow airport, pushed our way through a mob in the passport control line, whisked through customs, found our driver and translator, and were driven to our hotel. The hotel was an old Soviet hotel with sickles and hammers painted all over the place. We made it to our rooms after our passports were taken from us for "processing." Me? Scared? Why could you possibly think that?

Our room overlooked the Moskva River and the White House (yes, Russia has one too). I remember opening the window to cool down the room. (This was the only way to moderate the heat coming from the heated water pipes that pumped through the room for heat.) I just stared out the window and then instantaneously started to panic. What the hell was I doing? All of this rushing around, and it finally hit me that Jim and I were going to take two or three little humans home with us.

I could (and probably will) write a whole other book on the international adoption experience; however, I just wanted to focus on this specific point in time for me in the process. I thought I was going to vomit or faint or both. In that moment, I wanted to just run away and get on a plane and go back to the US. I kept thinking of how many times God had put it on my heart to take care of the orphans. At the same time, I was fighting my thoughts about how terribly unprepared I was to do all of this. I literally was driving my husband insane. Should we be doing this? What if this was a mistake? I know. A little late in the game for all of these doubts, but there was a flood of them. Not surprisingly, he left to take a walk through the hotel to chill out, and I was left staring at the wall or out the window.

I remember just crying and calling out to God. "I cannot do this. This is too big. This is too much of a responsibility. I am out." Then, in my silence, He reminded me that He had my back. He indeed got me into all of this and would help me through it. There were so many beautiful people who showed up for Jim and me through this process and donated clothing and toys. Our neighbors held a huge baby shower, as did some of our best friends. People prayed for us. Our parents had our backs and helped us financially. There was love and it was all around me. God just needed to point me in that direction again.

I started to think about the verse, "Perfect love casts out all fear." You know what? There is fear that needs to be cast out. It was not saying that I would be fearless. It was saying that there might be a ton of fear that I would feel, and perfect love would overcome it. Sometimes I think that I should not feel fear and, if I feel it, it means I do not have faith or enough love. We all feel fear, but what do we do with it? How is it overcome?

In my case, fear was overcome by God, and so many people loved and supported us. Did I still feel as though I was going to throw up the next day when we went into an office, and they handed us a folder with our three kids' files in it? ABSOLUTELY. I still was in a massive panic mode, but I pushed through it, knowing I was doing was God wanted me and Jim to do and knowing that His love and the love of those around me would drive out this fear that I was feeling. These kids would have a ton of love around them to be able to lessen their fears as well.

If my fears would have led me to get on that plane to go back to the US before adopting the kids, they would still be over there without a family, without a ton of love. My fear would have led to more fear, loneliness, and suffering for my kids. Have there been bumps in the road? Yeppers. But as my dad always taught me on the golf course, just focus on one shot at a time. Focus on the next step and making that a good one. This is such good advice not only on the course but throughout all of my life.

Let's take a quick look at the reverse of the quote from 1 John 4:18: "There is no love in fear. But perfect fear drives out love." I would submit that this is also true for all of us. There is no love in fear, and overwhelming fear will drive out all semblance of love and stability from one's life. Fear will limit what God wants us to do in our lives. Fear will limit our ability to love.

And I lived in fear for a long time in my spiritual life. I was afraid of God, so I could not love Him, myself, or others. My fear of dying led me to turn inward again and unable to effectively love. I was afraid of losing my dreams, having a lousy golf round, getting hurt, failing, being rejected, getting sick, and the list went on and on.

What do you think a fearful life looks like? I am glad you asked that question, because I can tell you—it looks an awful lot like stress, anxiety, depression, and addiction, and it feels like a failure. Imagine going from one thing to the next, searching for a sense of peace, and focusing inward with a plethora of emotional ups and downs. Oh, I think I did well today. Oops, not so good yesterday. I wonder if I will screw all of this up tomorrow?

There is no stability. Fear creates instability. I cannot focus on fear because then I become fearful and unloving. I cannot love others unconditionally and show them God's love and peace when I am racked with worry and instability.

What causes this instability? Not believing God. (Wow, we keep going back to this! It is like some kind of *theme* or something!) God is our stability. God's love is never changing. We need to trust this. His love does not waver, and when we believe in God's constant love in our lives, it brings a whole other level of steadiness and strength.

When we focus on love and therefore drive the fear out of our lives, we change. We do not search for approval and do not need material things to feel successful in what the world defines as success. Hurt does not destroy us, and it is possible to live with uncertainty. Because everything comes from God, we have stability. *"Peace I leave with you; my peace I give to you. I do not give to you as the world gives. Do not let your hearts be troubled, and do not let them be afraid"* (John 14:27). The world cannot give us anything as valuable as the love of God.

No more ups and downs. It is us and love and God.

And maybe you guessed it, but we become more like God when we focus on His love. (We will talk about this during the meditation chapter. It is amazing. Our brains literally change when we connect with God. And guess what? It also changes for the worse when we focus on fear.)

So, not only do we destroy our brain and revert to balls of panic and fear when we choose not to believe in God's unconditional love, but we also block our ability to spread His love to the world. We get so wrapped up in ourselves that we cannot see straight.

This fear of life and God also limits our ability to change. That is right—all of that fear is counterproductive. At the end of the day, fearing God hinders Him and us.

I started to think of this as surgery. Whatever is wrong with our body is inside us. We have to trust the surgeon to put us under anesthesia, open us up, fix our issues, close us up, allow us to recover, and ultimately, make us better. The surgeon is there for follow-up appointments and to track how we are doing.

God heals us in this way. If we let him get inside of us, see our sickness, trust Him to *do surgery*, and come to our follow up appointments, He can heal us. 😊

He changes us.

I do not perform my surgery or have the expertise to fix what went wrong in my body, nor can I fix the sins I created from the pain in my life. God has to heal the pain in me. I need to show up to receive treatment, open and committed to being cured. What if I never went to the hospital for my physical surgery? It means I would never get better. If I never show up to my relationship with God, He will not restore or cure me. I have to be present. Our choices are the ones that hinder God's ability to love us fully and enable us to love others. When we choose not to show up, we limit His movement in our lives.

We must consciously decide to let go and let God take over. Because of our egos, we sin. The more we try and tap into our ego to bring us out of sin, it pulls us further down and exacerbates the problem. It is impossible and illogical to rely upon our fallible selves.

It is only through our connection to God that we can truly become aware of our faults. Yes, everyone knows the sins, such as the Ten Commandments, but what about the other sins? We need to be able to see the nuances in our lives. Think about the Samaritan woman at the well. How did she realize her living situation was not ideal? Jesus told her. She did not figure this out before her encounter with Jesus.

How about Paul? His encounter with God changed him. Moses? The same. How about St. Augustine? He was once quoted as saying, "This is the very perfection of a man, to find out his own imperfections." And boy was he confronted by God about his addiction to women: "Oh Lord, give me chastity, but do not give it yet." At that point, St. Augustine was well aware that sleeping around was not a good thing, and he had to work through this with God.

None of these people would have become aware of their shortcomings without an encounter with God. Therefore, *fixing yourself, making yourself worthy, and presenting your soul to God when you are finished perfecting* tactic does *not* work. The approach is backward, and it is why so many people are frustrated. Therefore, the order needs to be:

- Form a rock-solid relationship with God and realize He loves you no matter what.

- Spend time in silence and listen to Him.

- Become more loving, more forgiving, more empathetic, and more merciful through Him.

If you have read stories about the saints, many of them mention the stronger their relationship was with God, and the more holy they became, they actually found more and more faults within themselves. And surprisingly enough, they were ecstatic about it. What the saints were able to grasp is our constant imperfections will be like a continuous game of Whack-A-Mole. One pain, hurt, or sin we knock out, and another one will appear. But since we know our Savior cares so deeply for us, this fact does not need to discourage us. The more time we spend with Jesus, the more we grow like Him. We have to focus on becoming a more compassionate soul. Daily feedback from our unconditional, loving God is a privilege. And the longer we cultivate this relationship, the more aware we will become of everything we do and our motivations, both good and bad.

This is repenting. We believe Jesus is our Savior, and in becoming closer to Him, we welcome and are open to having our hearts changed. *"Be still, and know that I am God."* (Psalms 46:10). The beauty of Jesus is that he is a wounded healer, and He understands us. We need to relate to Him this way, not as a Santa Claus or a Superman. He is a friend who accompanies us side-by-side because the world wounded Him too. Jesus understands the abandonment of friends, the frustration, the rejection, the temptation, the coworker issues, the broken bones, the disappointments, the pain—all of it. We need to relate to Him there. He is not *above us* in the sense that He does not know what it is like to struggle. He struggled tremendously His whole life.

I have noticed that in my life, I tend to gravitate to those who have struggled with the same things that I have. Their pain can be my redemption. Their stories and honesty can provide hope—just as Jesus' suffering is also my redemption. By His wounds, we are healed—not merely the scars of the crucifixion, but also the wounds of His life on earth.

Lastly, I want to touch quickly on a subject: our expectations of God. Many times our friendship with God wavers on our expectations surrounding Him and the events in our lives. To develop a genuine relationship with God, believe it or not, we need to love Him unconditionally. What does that even mean?

I think we all have been so focused on the love of God and the love we have for others as a transactional relationship. This is why we cannot get past the *"I am so awful, guilty, shameful, etc.,"* part of being a Christian. Every time someone brings up that God loves us unconditionally, it is almost immediately followed by some kind of "but." (As Pee-wee said in the *Pee-wee's Big Adventure* movie: "All my friends have big buts," but I digress.)[11] Seriously, we feel good for a moment in time and are 100% sure that God loves us, and then the hammer comes down. We spiral into a place of self-pity and frustration, thinking we will never be able to live up to the expectations that God supposedly puts on us.

In addition, we get upset when we ask God for things, but they do not come to fruition. We somehow feel as though we are *owed* because we have lived a good life and have helped others. All we have to do is look at the lives of the Apostles. Almost all of them died horrific deaths. They gave up their livelihoods, followed Jesus, met Jesus again after His Resurrection, spread the Good News, yet they were violently killed. If any people should have been given a break and some extra stars, it is this group of people. But alas, they were not.

We expect Him to love us unconditionally, but we do not reciprocate. (Note: why should we expect God to love us unconditionally if we do not even attempt to love Him unconditionally?) Most of us, including myself, tend to love God conditionally. We blame Him when our worlds do not work out the way we want them to. We reject Him when things do not go our way or suffer pain. God is there to love us like no other. He is not there to change our circumstances. All we need is to pray for strength to get through the bad times in our lives and not curse our Maker when things go sideways. God never said He would fix all of our troubles. He said He would be there with us in the middle of all of the chaos and lessen our burdens. Just like we would not expect our friends or family to produce miracles in our lives

---

11   Tim Burton, *Pee-Wee's Big Adventure* (1985; Burbank, CA: Warner-Brothers, 2000), DVD.

continually, we cannot assume God will swoop in and take away all of our pain.

We wonder why God would allow such terrible things to happen to people He loves so much. But He never promised us that nothing bad would happen to us or that He would always rescue us from suffering. This is a condition we put on our love of God. He never wanted that. He wants us to love Him unconditionally. We owe Him that. I can fall in love with a God who cares about me and loves me regardless. And I can love Him back regardless.

We all need to get off of this cyclical destructive relationship with God. On the one hand, we think we are not good enough and might get thrown into the bowels of hell when we pass away. On the other hand, we still have these feelings that somehow we are trying really hard and are better than other people, and our lives are in many levels of turmoil that are undeserved.

What if we took another look at this whole love thing and turned it on its head and stopped looking at everything concerning what we have or have not done and what God has or has not done. Let go of how much or how little we have sinned and what our life challenges are. We do not look for God to do anything. He is not our personal agent who will make everything better (or worse).

This then begs the question of what good is God? Why should we even care? What does He do for us? For one, He lets us live in freedom by getting off of the transactional roller coaster many of us are on. He is way more concerned with His relationship with us than with what we have or have not done. He wants us to be open to Him affecting our lives. He wants us to be free.

So, what is this freedom that Jesus offers? What is the Good News? Many people think the "Good News" is the Great Commandment of loving our neighbors as ourselves. That is technically "Old News." That is actually what we should have been doing all along, and it is discussed in the Old Testament.

The *"Good News"* is that Jesus showed us there is no transactional relationship between God and us anymore. It is not a tit-for-tat type of relationship. And as good as that sounds to us, it is also not a relationship in which our actions or inaction force God's hand to either give us everything we ask for because we are *good* or provide us with nothing because we are *bad*. In Matthew 5:45, we learned the sun shines on the good and the bad. God's love is everywhere, shining on everyone. The difference is, do we tap into this love? Do we take the time to have a connection with God? Is our relationship genuine, or are we still hanging on to the thought that God hates us for everything we have done? He wants us to be in a relationship with Him, which takes precedence over sin, brings us closer to God, and changes us. Unfortunately, many of us miss the boat that God simply wants us as we are. He loves us so much and wants us to find joy, peace, love, mercy, grace, forgiveness in the mess that is our lives.

God is the constant in our lives. Jesus is our friend, and His love is not going to change in intensity for us or others. This is a crucial point. To believe God should give us a better life means we assume we are better than other people around us who do not deserve better. It is not a contest. We do not know what other people have endured because we are all broken, and we should practice empathy for others and the circumstances that led to their struggles. Jesus loves them immensely, too, and wants to free them from their pain as well. He wants them to feel peace.

How do they find peace? They need a constant, non-transactional, non-judgmental love in their lives. They just need someone to see their core and be crazy in love with them regardless of the sin, pain, hurt, etc. They need to know that they have worth and are lovable. Most people in this world, believe it or not, do not think they are lovable, and they make many horrific life decisions based upon feeling worthless—addictions, affairs, suicide, etc. You name it, and many times, it is tied to feelings for worthlessness. Who can provide your worth? The Creator of the Universe. He loves you, regardless. It is time to believe this. It is time to let go of "conditional like" and genuinely believe in unconditional love.

This relationship with God is redeeming for us because it is different from the love that people provide us. No matter how crazy in love with us someone is, there are conditions baked in somewhere. Only in God will my soul find rest. Without God, we do not have a place of rest. We have nowhere to go. We have only our constant pining, searching, and clawing for someone here on earth to love us unconditionally but there remains a constant void. We are on an impossible journey and will forever be filled with disappointment. We need to be on a *possible* journey, and that is with our God. We are born with a God-shaped hole in our hearts. "You have made us for yourself, O Lord, and our hearts are restless until they rest in you."—St. Augustine

So, He heals us by providing stability, unwavering love, forgiveness, and peace. Then, we take all of this strength in our lives and provide stability for those around us.

For the longest time, I thought that God would always take care of me in the sense that everything would work out, and my path would be straight if I trusted in God. If I really had a ton of faith, things would go my way, or goodness and awesomeness would prevail. But as I grew older and have experienced more, I know this expectation is not accurate nor realistic. When we follow the Gospels, life is better, but there is not immunity to problems. It has become one of my pet peeves when people say that things always happen for the best. Really? Tell that to child sex slaves in India (or in America for that matter) who end up dead in sewers at the innocent age of ten. I worked for a few years at an international NGO that focused on liberating people from all forms of modern-day slavery. We had a meeting every day in which everyone from headquarters gathered to pray for all of our cases and efforts around the world. Some of the shared stories were horrific.

There is no happy ending for all of these situations and no good reason these events happen. So, what does it really mean to trust God in our lives? While most of our lives will never see the level of tragedy others might experience, we nevertheless have trials. We have the health issues, the abuse, the broken hearts, the lost jobs, the out-of-control children, the addictions, the betrayals—the list is endless. So, what does trusting and believing in God mean in these situations? To be sure, it is not trusting in the best possible outcome. For every example that I can provide where a miracle happened, there are about 100 times it did not. I do not mean to sound like a downer, but we need to start viewing our relationship with God a little differently—He is with us and loves us no matter what, in all circumstances. That is it. That is all that we can trust.

I will never forget the chance encounter I had at the Cleveland Hopkins International Airport one afternoon. My flight came in early, and I was waiting for my parents to arrive to pick me up. They were running a little late, and so I sat myself down on a bench close to the rotating doors on the arrivals level of the airport. Being the introvert that I am, I took out a book and tried not to make eye contact with anyone so they would not want to engage in a conversation. I already had a long discussion on the plane with another passenger, and I was all talked out.

"Hi, how are you doing today?" a very kind man asked as he sat down next to me. He had a nametag on, so I knew he worked at the airport. "I am on a quick break."

Oh, no! I thought to myself. I am not ready to have yet another conversation.

"Hi," I mustered enough energy to say to him. And then the conversation flowed. He went on and on about his family and his work at the airport. And then, the conversation took a dark turn. He lived in a rather rough section of town with his extended family, many of whom recently had serious health issues or were killed or in jail. One member of his family had stolen some money from him. He was worried about his daughter and her questionable boyfriend. As we talked, the tragedies kept piling up. In the back of my mind, I kept thinking that I had no idea how this person made it through every day. I listened to him, and somehow, I thought in a holier-than-thou way that I contributed to his life simply by being there for him.

"Well, my break is over, " he said as he got up from the bench and started to walk away. But then he turned around, looked me straight in the eye, and said, "And you know what?"

"What?" I was curious.

"God is so good. He has just been so good to me throughout my entire lifetime. He loves me so incredibly much, and it makes me so happy and at peace."

Mic drop. I almost fell off the bench.

Here I thought that God put me on that bench to be there for this kind man who had endured some of life's hardest moments. In reality, this man provided me a whole new perspective about our experiences and God's love for us. They are not tied together. You can still be close to God as the world is falling apart around you. You are okay, and God is still good.

Every time I think of that man, tears come into my eyes. He was so filled with God's joy in the midst of hardship. I knew that was the kind of relationship I wanted with God. That is so life-giving and can change others' lives, just like this man changed mine.

What does this have to do with Jesus dying on the cross for our sins? How is this all related? Jesus, even through all of

His suffering, was not *attached* to anything. He did not seek riches and endured the rejection of people and faced terrible trials. Yes, Jesus, God's Son, was let down by friends and handed over to be crucified by one of His disciples, Judas. By all accounts, Jesus was a failure. When he died, he probably only had a few hundred followers. He was tempted with worldly desires. He got frustrated at life, at his disciples, and dare I say, even at His Father. In Luke 22:42, He said, *"Father, if you are willing, remove this cup from me; yet, not my will but yours be done."* But He prayed. He stayed focused on His love for others and God and simply worked to set people free.

That is the "Good News" and God Awe-Fullness—a better, more centered way of life—forgiveness when we fail, release from our shortcomings and attachments, unconditional love, mercy, and grace. In short, happiness and peace.

••• 6 •••
Shhhhh—God Is Talking to You—Can You Hear Him?

Meditation is always becoming. Meditation is always transformation. Meditation always moves us from one place to another; from unconsciousness to awareness, from tension to relaxation, from being scattered to being centered, from a shallow relationship with our environment and ourselves to a deeper one, from sleep to wakefulness, from a sense of God's absence to the sense that God was in this place all along and I didn't know it!

—Alan Lew

I HAVE ALWAYS wanted to visit Italy, and though I have not had the chance to go there yet, my close friends went and took a ton of pictures. They were so excited about their trip and in old-school fashion, printed all of their pictures and put them in two substantial artsy-craftsy binders. (Yeah, my photos from my life are scattered all over the place. This made me feel like a failure from the beginning of our gathering. But I digress.) My husband and I went over to their house for dinner. We were enjoying the evening conversation and stories of their travels, then it happened. All of a sudden, it was time to walk through the two huge binders—picture by picture.

Somebody help me. *Seriously, help me.*

Their faces were lit up the entire three hours we sat and listened to all of the elaborate stories that corresponded to each of the photos—every single solitary one of them. Even though I really wanted to go to Italy (and still do), none of this really excited me. I was trying to connect to an experience that I had not yet had. My eyes glazed over as I fake-smiled and politely nodded throughout the presentation. Then, we said our goodbyes. I was thrilled they had such a wonderful time, and I was glad I was there for them to share their amazing memories.

It struck me, though, how seeing pictures and hearing about others' experiences are definitely not the same thing as experiencing those things for ourselves. This holds true for our relationship with God. Many of us spend a ton of time attending church, prayer groups, and classes. We read religious books and listen to spiritual music. But are we really listening to God, or are we only hearing Him? We can hear others' experiences with God, but we cannot fully experience the Creator of the Universe for ourselves until we connect directly with God and listen to Him. Short of that we will be trying to live our spiritually through other people's eyes. Boring. "You can't color your world with someone's paint."—Israelmore Ayivor

What about your experiences with God?

I would submit that many of us are scared to sit in silence and listen to God. It can be uncomfortable when we start, and we might find ourselves running away, finding distractions, reading, surfing the internet, or making a third cup of tea—anything that will let us put this off for one more day. We do not make an effort to know God more intimately because we do not have the time. Or what I more commonly find is we are scared of what that encounter might uncover, and we do not trust our experience of God. It is easier to listen to someone else tell us what they learned from listening to God as opposed to us having the confidence to believe that yes, God is really communicating with us, and we can trust this experience.

I used to work at a Christian non-profit where we had a half-hour prayer time built into our workday. It was a great place to work. However, I noticed that 95% of the people there would fill that half-hour of quiet time with anything but absolute silence. They started prayer groups, read, listened to podcasts, and did anything but be still and be quiet. Why? Many told me that they struggled to sit in silence with God. It can be scary, but boy, it is so powerful when you meet the challenge to be quiet with God.

We need to be silent to hear that faint voice inside us that is drowned out by the daily deluge of noise, technology, and responsibilities and, instead, be comfortable in His presence. We need to feel accepted by Him to be quiet with Him. We need to break out of our daily busyness to stop hearing our voice and start listening to His.

The best way to know God is to be quiet and listen and trust what we hear. Sometimes, it will be nothing that we can verbalize afterward. I tell you, though, that God is working in you even when you do not feel it or cannot explain it.

> God is working in you even when you do not feel it or cannot explain it.

Besides, we cannot change and become more compassionate and more empathetic human beings without this alone time with our ultimate friend. As much as we would like to think it is sheer willpower to change into a more compassionate person, it is not. Our brains were built for the connection with God through meditation. How do we know this? The areas of our brains that allow us to be compassionate get larger the more we meditate.

We Were Built for This

The book, *How God Changes Your Brain* by Andrew Newberg, M.D. and Mark Robert Waldman, is a very eye-opening read. [12] In a nutshell, studies have revealed that God is part of our consciousness, and the more we think about God, the more we will modify the neural circuitry in particular sections of the brain. The authors say that when we meditate on God over a long time, we permanently alter the structure of our minds that regulate our moods, provide our sense of self, and form our sensory experiences.

In addition to the health benefits that meditation provides (ex. decreasing anger, keeping the mind young, regulating emotions, etc.), regular meditation makes us more compassionate. There is a catch here, though—we cannot only meditate a few minutes here and there and expect to change our brains. We need to commit to meditating for more extended periods of time on a consistent basis to reap the benefits, physically, emotionally, and spiritually. Newberg and Waldman saw in their studies that people who meditate for 30 minutes a day for many years show the most change in their neural activity.

Okay, please do not put the book down after reading this. I remember when I started the Ignatian Spiritual Exercises and was told that I needed to find an hour a day for reading, contemplation, and prayer for the next 30 weeks. Trust me, I was scared and overwhelmed, but when I started to work this

---

12   Newberg and Waldman, *How God Changes Your Brain*.

time into my day, I did not want to miss it. I looked forward to spending part of my day with God, and over time, I started to see the changes in my day-to-day life.

A little bit of tough love here: We cannot be surprised if we do not find God's peace if we do not put in the time. *"Do not worry about anything, but in everything by prayer and supplication with thanksgiving, let your requests be made known to God. And the peace of God, which surpasses all understanding, will guard your hearts and your minds in Christ Jesus"* (Philippians 4:6-7). It would be like expecting to shoot 71 in golf (an excellent score) without ever touching a golf club, making straight As without studying, or winning a nationally televised talent show without practice or vocal lessons. There are a ton of videos on YouTube of people who try out for these talent shows and think they can compete without effort. I am not saying that our spiritual lives are a competition. However, the people who can feel God's peace and love are the ones who spend the most time with Him. That actually makes sense. If we do not spend a lot of time with God, we will not feel His love or His peace. And to be quite honest, we should not expect to.

I now understand why I was able to change, despite myself, when I spent a lot of time in meditation. I was able to hear God speaking to my soul loud and clear in the silence. But I was also exercising my brain, in a sense, to become better able to be empathetic and to quash the natural anger response in certain situations. Anger, as one can surmise, destroys the brain, so being able to regulate that emotion is critical to our health.

Not only was I able to hear God, but I was able to listen to myself think. It was undeniable that I had drowned out my thinking with all of the world's distractions—the TV, the smartphone, the radio, work, hobbies, and other people. Yes, we can be there for other people, but we need to find time for ourselves. Even Jesus had to get away from everyone and focus on listening to God. He was fully human and fully divine and needed to find the time to talk to God. Think about that for a few minutes. The Son of God needed time away from everything and everyone to hear Himself think and connect with His Father. 'Nuff said.

When my soul started to be more and more in contact with God, my perspective on life started to change. My actions changed, and I did not have to do all of this through my willpower. A lot of things in my life that were insanely important became less critical. I became more patient with my kids (not totally patient, but more so). I let go of some grudges. (I am still working on a few more to let go.) The bottom line is I am slowly transforming through my relationship with God. So, developing my relationship with God has come first before the changes in my life. Am I done changing? Absolutely not. Not even close. The closer I become to God, the more aware I become of my inadequacies. That is okay because I *want* to find more weaknesses at this point in my life because I know that God can help me overcome them and draw closer to Him. At the end of the day, that is what I want the most—to be as intimate as I can with my all-loving Creator.

Another benefit of connecting with God is we can make decisions agnostic to what everyone else is doing. We make decisions out of the loving part of ourselves that knows our true desires. We need to be still to see clearly. Getting to know love is getting to know God. Loving yourself also means getting in touch with that love in your life and choosing to live out of that place. If you do not love yourself, you have not met God. Let me say that again. If you do not love yourself, you have not truly connected with God in a direct personal relationship.

We need the big *I Am* to meet our smaller I am. I meet God in the present where there is no sin in the past or future. My time with Him is just His presence meeting my presence. I need to be in the present to be able to meet the Almighty

God. He is nowhere else. This is why mercy and forgiveness flow so perfectly from God. We always have a chance for our *I am* to meet His *I Am* in the stillness of the moment.

It really struck me when reading about mystics and saints that they did not tend to spend an inordinate amount of time learning from books. They always speak of connecting to God in their hearts. Jesus tells us that God is Love. We connect with Him on the love level. I cannot connect with a God of love by simply thinking about Him. I need to love Him. The more I take the time to know His love for me, the more I can love Him and other people. If all I do is think about Him, He will still love me, but the connection will not be as strong.

So, then how do we connect with God? How can you get the benefits of meditating? What is the best way of meditating? According to Newberg and Waldman, as well as many other authors, there are many ways to meditate. Many of the forms include music, a mantra, and/or breathing—some incorporate movement. You can actually meditate while you are walking.

However, since there are so many forms of meditation and I cannot go into all of them here, I would like to focus on a few types of prayer that I use that have been beneficial to me: meditation, contemplation, the Examen, and writing.

Meditation

Depending on who you read, there are various ways to meditate, and that is wonderful. Anything that can get people to be quiet and still their mind is a great thing. Many forms of meditation have people focus on relaxing their bodies, following their breath, focus on loving-kindness, and the list goes on. I have used a lot of those techniques, and they are incredible for relaxing, sleeping, calming anxiety, becoming more reflective, loving, and open. For me to connect to God, I use a simple meditation technique to center myself, be still, and listen to God. I empty my mind as much as I can and just sit in the silence. Although this is the most simple, it can be a little challenging at first because there is not much to it. It is easy to get in your head and think: *Could I be cleaning the house? Could I be exercising? Could I be writing this book? What else could I be doing? When did just being become a big ole waste of time?*

The other challenging part of sitting still with God is that all of the distractions in my life are gone—no TV, no music, no phone—nothing. That is when all those thoughts I shoved down bubble up to the surface, but I do not need to address them at that time. I pledge to myself I will set them aside during my meditation time.

During my time with God, the objective for me is to be able to listen, be still, and be quiet. And after frequently meditating over an extended period, those thoughts work themselves out. You have to trust this.

I use a few techniques during meditation when random thoughts or worries strike (and they will strike for everyone). The first is picking one word at the beginning of my practice and using that word to draw me back to silence. So, sometimes I choose *trust, love, peace, grace*, or something like that. Many times, I sit in silence for a few minutes to see what word comes to mind. So, every time something pops into my head, I use the word to refocus.

The second technique is to name the distraction and let it go. For example, if I am stressing out about work, I simply say *work* in my mind and let the thought go. This would be the same for other worries—finances, kids, friends, etc. For some reason, naming the thought seems to allow me to let it go out of my head.

So, the goal is to sit with God and be present. Even if I sit and *hear* nothing for my 30 minutes, it is not a waste of time because I am hanging out and spending time with God. Just like I can hang out with people I know well and simply be in their presence, I can do the same with God. He wants us to do this. For some reason, I used to feel as though my prayer time was not productive unless I thanked God for things, asked Him for things, read the Bible, etc. These are excellent ways of building a foundation of our faith, but to be close to God, we need to take the next step and be willing just to be present with Him. We need to stop thinking about Him and be able to feel Him in our hearts.

Do not be surprised that we can *listen* to God through our connections with our souls in the silence. I have had some of my greatest clarity in the quiet. God speaks to me there. This may or may not happen with you. God has many ways of communicating in silence with people. I am just letting you know of my experiences if they can help you out just a bit. Do not get discouraged. Just like we need to practice anything to get better, the ability to sit in silence will take time. Stick with it.

There are many meditation resources out there for people to explore, and I would encourage you to look and find what works for you. However, be cautious that you do not pick a technique that involves a lot of thinking and following others' instructions for the entire time. You need some time to be silent and connect to God, who loves you so incredibly much. Set a timer and just be still.

Contemplation

When I think of contemplation, I think of focusing all of my thoughts on God. So, unlike meditation, where I sit in silence, contemplation is more active and complementary to meditation. There are usually two approaches that I draw upon. First, I spend some time putting myself into a Biblical scene and see what unfolds. I want to work to notice everything in the scene: What do I look like? What does the scene smell like? What is the weather? How many people are in the scene with me? What am I saying? With whom am I engaging? How am I feeling? How am I acting/reacting? I read the passage, then absorb myself in the scene, and then reread the passage.

The second approach I have taken is to take one verse of the Bible and merely focus on that. For example, *"Peace I leave with you; my peace I give to you; not as the world gives do I give to you. Let not your hearts be troubled, neither let them be afraid"* (John 14:17). I will sit and think of this phrase. What if I believed this 100%, not 50%? What would my life look like if I were *all in?* How would my day-to-day be different? Why don't I let myself believe this?

The Examen

So, for a quick prayer during my day, I turn to the Examen. It only takes about ten minutes to do, and to me, there is nothing more accessible for me to use to do a quick check-in with myself and really evaluate the events of the day. The Examen is a type of prayer that is part of Ignatian spirituality and is introduced in the Ignatian Exercises. However, you do not need to know anything about the Ignatian Exercises to utilize the Examen in your life.

So, the Ignatian Exercises were created by St. Ignatius. Who is this St. Ignatius? St. Ignatius was a Catholic priest and theologian and was one of the co-founders of the Jesuits. There is a lot of material out there if you want to know more about this fascinating human being and his spiritual development. The Examen that he created is a group of reflective prompts to use to reflect on our every day and provides insight into our spirit and our interactions with God and others. (As a side note, I know there can be a lot of divisiveness when the Jesuits are mentioned. People either love them or hate them. I do not want you to be distracted by the fact that the Examen is from St. Ignatius. There is nothing controversial about being grateful to God and reviewing your day with Him.)

The five sections of the Examen include the following:

1. Gratitude
2. Review
3. Response
4. Desire
5. Hope

The first section, gratitude, involves just that. What are you grateful for today? What happened in the last 24 hours that caused you to be highly aware of God's presence in the world and love for you? Even the simple practice of doing this every day will change the way you look at your life. You will begin to see that you are indeed blessed even amid the chaos. You will also be more aware of where God is showing up in your life, and you might just not be taking the time to notice and be grateful.

The second section is review your day. What was good about it? What did not go so well? This is where it is majorly important to know you are in a safe space, both with yourself and with God. You can look at the awesomeness and the ugliness at the same time. You can also become aware of how you feel. Are you wickedly stressed out? Are you at peace? What is causing you to feel how you feel? How are you responding to specific people during the day? Why are you angry at someone? How can this be resolved? This is where you become aware of how your days are truly going.

Third, you look at your responses to these ups and downs of the day. How did you respond to your successes? Why did you react in a certain way to a situation? How did you fall short in being the person you wanted to be?

The fourth part of the Examen is desire. Looking forward to the new day, how would you like God to accompany you to assist you in your weaknesses and capitalize on your strengths? How can you respond to those around you in a more productive way? How can you respond to yourself in a more life-giving, positive way?

And, finally, you close with hope. Ask God to help you in any way you need His assistance. He is your friend. Ask Him to walk beside you over the next day and make you more aware of His love, forgiveness, grace, mercy, and hope.

When you do this prayer regularly, you will start to notice patterns (good and bad) in your life. It is quite eye-opening, trust me.

Writing

I will admit that some of my most significant breakthroughs have come from writing. I know a lot of people do not like to write, and that is more than okay. Writing will not be your thing. But this kind of writing could be, if you give it a chance.

You see, the writing that has benefited me the most is simply the kind where I sit down at my computer and write whatever comes into my head. It is a stream of consciousness writing. I do not edit anything (even dark thoughts, swearing, etc.) I edit nothing. I just keep writing whatever is popping into my head.

I will admit that when I started doing this, I was petrified. Should I put some of these thoughts on paper or in a file on my computer? Honestly, you could write stuff out and then delete it or tear up the paper if you want. You will be surprised at what you write. I guarantee it. But you have to commit to a time and solely write during that time. No edits. No proper grammar. Nothing. Just write what you are thinking. As weird as this sounds, your soul and deep feelings that you have show up if you are courageous enough to do this. I personally look at this as another type of prayer. To be honest with all of you, this book would never have been written without hours of meditation and stream of consciousness writing. I became aware of so much in my life when I stopped editing it.

Connection with God

> I became aware of so much in my life when I stopped editing it.

All of this talk about being in God's presence brought me back to something my parents (and many others) burned into my brain as I was growing up: "Who you surround yourself with, you become." So, if you take the time to surround yourself in God's presence, you will access that quiet voice inside of you, and you will become more like Him—not perfect, but *wicked good*. If you surround yourself with noise, technology, and a constant barrage of people attached to the world, you will become more like them. And if you sit around talking down to yourself all day with your negative voice inside your head, you will become more like what that little negative voice is telling you.

I am reminded of when my husband and I went to Sonoma, California, for our 25th Anniversary trip. One day it was raining outside, and he decided to take a nap. I started a fire in the fireplace in the room and just sat and watched the flames flicker. I was looking to meditate for a while in the warmth of the fire. As I was sitting and listening to God, I heard a thump and a piece of the main log broke off and fell to the bottom of the fireplace, still on fire. I began to think about how this relates to our meditation and prayer times with God. We spend time being one with Unconditional Love, and then we break off (so to speak) at the end of the meditation time to go through our day, and we are still on fire.

We need this conversation with our Creator to become a louder and louder part of our lives. For many of us, including myself, our connection with God is too drowned out by all of the daily noise. And when we are stressed or upset, we add to the noise by distracting ourselves so that the voice inside becomes even fainter, even less clear. We have to resist the temptation for distraction and, instead, come to God as the lovable creation we are, worthy of a relationship with Him. He wants us to feel that. And this needs to be louder than the stress, the crazy, and the noise. It cannot be louder if we do not attend to it; if there is no time for it.

The closer we become to God, the more our vision for the world will change. We will be the sheep and not the goats (Matthew 25:31-46). The goats never saw Jesus in the people around them. The sheep who were close to the shepherd did. They saw the world differently. We can all see the world and ourselves in a very different way. And it is in knowing Him more intimately that the fear subsides. Fearing the God who loves you can only mean that you do not know Him well enough.

Commit to spending time with Him. Do this for yourself. It will change your entire life.

Part 3

EMBRACING THE ART OF IMPERFECTION— MAKING YOUR STUMBLES PART OF THE DANCE

··· 7 ···

Imperfecting Your Palette— Separating Out the Black from the Bright and Getting Rid of the Grey

Without black, no color has any depth. But if you mix black with everything, suddenly there's shadow — no, not just shadow, but fullness. You've got to be willing to mix black into your palette if you want to create something that's real.

—Amy Grant

HOW DO OUR imperfections weave their way into our lives, and how does God utilize all of these missteps and redeem them for impact in this world? I like to think of concepts

visually, and when I thought of God working with our imperfections, I kept coming back to the idea of painting with
colors and the beauty in all different types of art.

Unfortunately, for a long time, I thought the world was
basically black and white. Life did not include any real vibrant
colors. Everything and everyone (including myself) were
either good or bad. I always tried to stay in the background,
covering up the darkness in my life, and at the same time, not
really feeling worthy of acknowledging I was a pretty good
person in other areas in my life. I started to love being *grey*—
not quite bad and not quite good.

I even noticed this philosophy in my wardrobe, believe
it or not. I realized a few years ago that I tended to gravitate
toward the color of grey for my clothing. This color never
drew too much attention to myself, and it was always wear-
able with jeans. No brainer. It meant I did not even have to
think ahead about what to pair anything with. Grey slowly
began to dominate my wardrobe. I remember going to the
store one day, where I picked up a bunch of new tops and was
so excited to have found a ton that I liked! Then, I looked at
them again—they were all grey. So much for a new wardrobe!

There is a downside to basic grey. It is neither hot nor
cold, dark nor light—only sits in-between. No one is drawn
to it or repelled by it. Has anyone ever said their favorite color
in the whole wide world is grey?

I remember hearing the song "Grey Street" by the Dave
Matthew's Band for the first time, and I was drawn to it
immediately.[13] The song is about a woman whose colors blend
together into grey. She lost herself, wondering how she got to
such an empty place in life. What happened to her opinions
and her dreams? She craves to start over after burning her life
to the ground. She wants to be living in bright colors and get

---

13   Dave Matthews Band, "Grey Street," track 2 on *Busted Stuff*, RCA
Records, 2002, compact disc.

rid of the grey. In the end, she could not make this change. Her brilliant life continues to be subdued by the darkness, keeping her in the proverbial grey.

You see, at that time, I was really struggling with where my life was headed. My job was not fulfilling to me, and I was not really doing anything fun I loved. I did not have a lot of close friends, and I was hiding. I never really let anyone get really close to me, and I never spoke up to say what I truly wanted. No one *really knew* me or saw me for who I was. In reality, I did not even see me for who I was for fear of judgment. I was in a massive protective mode with other people and with God.

When we run and hide from ourselves and try to squash our *badness* down, we end up also squashing our goodness. All the colors mix to grey. When I did this, I became boring. I became bland. I became dead inside.

When we accept ourselves as we are because we know that God accepts us, good and bad, we can really start living and grow in our relationship with God. *"I praise you, for I am fearfully and wonderfully made. Wonderful are your works; that I know very well"* (Psalms 139:14). Yeah, we might have some darkness in us, but we have brilliant reds, yellows, blues, greens, pinks, and purples. And we color the world with all of these beautiful shades. When we meditate and reflect on God and listen to our souls, we begin to realize we have all of these different pigments to our lives, and God can help us heal our areas of darkness and work with us to make our areas of light glow. I dare say that God redeems our darkness and makes it beautiful. He works with all of our colors.

To make ourselves shine and to be able to do God's work, we need to accept our shadow side and allow Him to work there. If we don't, we will go grey. Our brilliance will be hidden right along with our weaknesses.

Just think how much brighter our lives will be if God genuinely sees us. What a weight off of our shoulders and gift to the world. We owe it to ourselves and the world to let God love us. Anything less, my friends, is entirely selfish. By trying to be perfect and hiding our weaknesses from everyone, we focus on ourselves—our reputation, our salvation, our lives. We are not thinking about how God wants to use us to interact with the world. This is all about God, not about us. We have to be willing to let all of the *us* go and allow *Him* to work through us.

This is freedom when we understand that no one and nothing can hurt us when we focus on letting the world know about God. When we are so overwhelmed by His love for us, nothing else matters. *Nothing.* When we are in that place, we are free to love, make mistakes, and learn from them. In that space, we can love others in their pain and suffering and understand them because we have taken the time to understand ourselves.

The more I have meditated, the more I have seen all sides of myself. And you know what? I started to see all of the sides of other people—everyone was not all good or all bad. They held both greatness and sometimes not so much greatness, which I finally understood.

I finally started to understand that this is how God sees me. He understands why I struggle in certain areas of my life and knows I have dark places. In Him, He redeems my sins, sees my strengths in a brighter light, and heals me so that I become a more connected person every day to God. And as I grow closer to God, I find my colors and God's are impossible to separate. God's love and my love become one. He forgives me, and I forgive others. Jesus' pain redeemed me, and my pain can help save others in their suffering. God and I become impossible to divide. These are my true colors.

Please note that I am not saying I am God. Nothing can be farther from the truth. However, I do believe that the Holy Spirit and the Creator of the Universe dwell in my soul. I need to unleash Him within me and not leave Him squashed and hidden. And of course, the more I know of God's love, the more able I am to show that love in my life to those around me.

So, by now, you must have figured out that the more we have our lives fade into grey, the less God can work through us. You squash you; you squash God.

Don't crush God!

One of the most fun times in my life was taking a drawing class with my mom. Every week we would show up and put our drawing horses (yes, that is what they are called) in a circle around what we were going to draw. And we would spend the next few hours going through the process of drawing, shading, fixing, etc. All of our drawings looked different, but they were of all the same object. "I paint the darkness and the silence. You see them as stars and poetry." —Jenim Dibie

This leads me to think about how we see ourselves and how God sees us. If I were in a room with God and painted a picture representing my life, and I did as well, what would be the main differences? For me, God's painting of my life would be much brighter, bolder, and happier. It would have a lot less of the black and more vivid and more unique colors. He would bring out my gifts, my joys, and my love by redeeming my flaws. The painting of my life would definitely have those bold colors, but it would have a lot more gray and black in there, as I still struggle in some areas of my life.

The big downer of this analogy is that many of us do not even see our paintings or God's. We look at our lives with the lights off, or we do not even take two seconds out of our lives to take an honest look at our strengths and weaknesses—our imperfect, magnificent selves. We don't even want to face the beauty of our lives because we are so afraid of the darkness that we might see. The courage to

We don't even want to face the beauty of our lives because we are so afraid of the darkness that we might see.

look honestly at our lives can come from believing that God loves us, no matter what kind of a mess of everything that we have made.

God's Palette—The Miraculous Happy Trees

> Despite my incessant desperation, I simply cannot paint the perfect picture within which I would wish to live out my life. And because I cannot, God picked up the brush of love, positioned the canvas of history and painted a manger.

—Craig D. Lounsbrough

When I was growing up, I used to watch Bob Ross on the TV. Yes, the happy trees guy. I will tell you that I was probably a pretty uptight kid and wanted everything to be perfect. It really made me nervous, watching the creative process or creating art—drawing, painting, or playing my guitar. I wanted everything to be perfect all the time. Approaching art as a perfectionist made me not want to try so I could avoid mistakes.

I can remember when I played Bach's "Cello Suite No. 1" on my classical guitar in front of a packed church. I was in my early 20s and rather new to performing classical pieces with an audience not only listening to the beauty of the music but, in my mind, also judging me. There was a section of the Cello Suite in which I started to fumble a little. I could feel the sweat starting to run down my forehead and panic washed over me. *I have so screwed this up! People will think this sounds awful.* Mass ended, and I ran into my friends and family at the back of the church. *Wow, that was so beautiful!* Everyone seemed to love it. I mentioned to a few people that I really thought I blew it. They seriously had no idea what I was talking about.

Those missed notes were simply part of my performance of one of Bach's masterpieces. I was trying so hard to be perfect that I missed the beauty of the music while I was playing it.

And then there was Bob Ross. He was on TV painting and was comfortable allowing his mistakes to be broadcast to the world. If something was a little off here and there, he found a way to blend it into the painting. When the painting was finished, and the cameras focused on it, you never had a clue there were errors. I was always intrigued by this idea. The mistakes were simply part of the beautiful, finished picture. The ultimate painter was always able to use the mistakes— either by blending them in somehow or by getting a better idea and improving on the original design.

God is like our own personal Bob Ross. ☺ (I know this sounds weird, but bear with me.) God does not control us, but He works with us to design an incredible life and redeem our mistakes and pain. He makes our stumbles part of the dance. He makes our blunders beautiful trees.

Soul painting includes your entire palette. You cannot leave out the bad because that is also what God redeems and uses to make your soul more truly yours and more beautiful. Nothing is left out.

We really need to look at the fact that God does redeem our indiscretions, pain, suffering, and disappointments, etc., and weaves these into the tapestry that is our soul. I have always tried to look back (and I get stuck there many times) on things I have done in the past I am ashamed of. It is not my job to redeem those events. It is my job to learn from them, become a better person, and have God help me inter-lace their lessons. Sometimes we cannot know or see what the lessons are, which is part of the harshness of life. When there is no clear insight to be discovered, the movement of our souls should be toward total reliance on God. Nothing on this planet will make us happy except His love. Nothing—no person, property, fame, success—nothing.

So, for all of those times I fell short in my relationship with God that I have so uncomfortably revealed to all of you reading this, I bet some of those shortcomings eventually helped me deal with relationship issues, career failures, spiritual struggles, impatience with my kids, etc. In my case, I think there were so many things that went wrong in my life all at once that it forced me to re-evaluate my spirituality. I know if everything had gone perfectly, I would never have written this book. I guess it is up to you to know whether that is a good thing or not.

If you are anything like me, the more I struggle, the more I appreciate those who struggle around me. I believe I used to be a lot more judgmental. Marriage issues? Who has those? Well, that is until I had some of my own. Wanting to walk away from God? Who would do that? I found out I wanted to walk away when everything started to go wrong. I was done with God for a while in my 20s, even though I was still in the pew every Sunday. I was mad. Now I can understand and talk to people who are in that place. Chronic pain? Been there, done that. It is so frustrating when people could not see the pain I was in, but I did not want to walk around and broadcast it. You know what? Now I understand people who are in pain.

If we are close to God, He provides us the ability to empathize with others who struggle as we do. It opens our hearts and allows us to love a little more unconditionally. We become more like God through our experiences of not being like God. Our imperfection is redeemed and leads us to unconditional love, which is God. Weird, huh?

People who believe they are perfect are awful empathizers. Really. Have you met someone who thinks they are perfect? They are maddening. They not only do not have a hint of compassion in their souls, but they also block their ability to become better. Take, for instance, the reality shows that have an expert come into an eating establishment to help them improve. When the owners of the establishment tell the expert that they are fantastic and perfect the way they are, absolutely no progress is made, and everyone is insanely frustrated. It is a waste of time. Only when the owners and the chefs in the establishment admit they are imperfect can real growth genuinely occur.

We create our life *with* God. We have Him work with our strengths and our weaknesses and our sins to move us toward our true selves. Our true selves are more and more able to show God's love and compassion every day. He redeems the pain and suffering others cause us. When He died for our sins, He also died to save us from the sins of others. God entwines those lessons and pain in our paintings as well. I alone cannot redeem my shortcomings and ease the suffering I cause other people, and many times, other people cannot ease the pain that they have caused me.

We are all broken. But by God (literally), we are all incredibly beautiful.

Turn on the lights and look at your painting and the painting God did of your life so far! Look at the piece of art you have become! Look at the strengths and weaknesses of others, know they are inherently good, and try the best they can with where they are. Be empathetic. Be courageous enough to do this.

Remember: Human perfection is relative, and so is imperfection. God painting with us does not make our paintings more perfect, but it makes the paintings more *us*, who we *really* are. God can redeem our mistakes and can truly help us understand who we are apart from who the world sees us (or how we think the world sees us). Our life paintings are always imperfect and are always beautiful, but they are genuinely a reflection of our true souls, our true selves.

I remember as a little kid, I went to the Smithsonian's Museum of Modern Art. I was overwhelmed at all of the styles of paintings, sculptures, statues, etc. What amazed me the most, though, was one particular painting. It was on a pressed wood board that looked like someone picked it up at the local home improvement store. The red stamps were still on the board, and there were two splashes of paint, one red and one blue. Why in the world is this in the museum? As a ten-year-old kid, all I could think was I could have created that in about 20 seconds. I am sure people with more art knowledge saw a lot more in that painting than I did. All of the art there was beautiful in some way, and each artist loved their artwork, and they knew who they were.

After viewing my life as a painting God and I are putting together on a day-to-day basis, it hit me that I cannot be one to judge what other people's life paintings look like. God does that. However, I can love people as unconditionally as I can and encourage them to open their hearts to a relationship with God. Every soul deserves a chance to grow closer to their Creator. Andre Gide once stated, "Art is a collaboration between the artist and God and the less the artist does, the better."

··· 8 ···

God, My Choreographer— The Everyday Dance with God (Stumbles and All)

Look at how a single candle can both defy and define the darkness.

—Anne Frank

WHEN MY HUSBAND, Jim, was 20, he went to Medjugorje, Yugoslavia, with his father as part of a pilgrimage. When they came home, Jim told me of the night they were outside and saw a brilliant light coming from a hill. The brightness was staggering. What was this light? Was there a great fire on the hill? What was happening? They had not seen anything like that before, so they decided to investigate.

A group of them trudged up the side of the hill and followed the illumination. Its brilliance did not waver. Finally, the group got there. What was the source of all of the brilliant light?

One. Single. Candle.

No matter how dark the world can get, it cannot lessen a single candle's radiance. However, I fear that we sometimes let it. Because we do not want to face our deficiencies, we also do not look at our strengths. We want to hide because if we put ourselves out there, people might see our weaknesses and know we are flawed. So, we hide. We extinguish our candles and curse the darkness.

I did that for a long time. How could I tell others about God if I was in total disarray at times? If I truly loved God, my Type A personality told me I should be able to get my crap together and be perfect. And, alas, I failed. Every single day I failed. I was not worthy of showing other people God's love.

Read that again: I felt I was not worthy of showing other people God's love.

And then, it hit me. This is not about me at all. My ability to point others to God has nothing to do with my previous failings or successes. It has everything to do with the fact that God's incredible love is unconditional and unchanging and for everyone. He has taken all of the ups and downs in my life and made them work for His good. He redeemed all of my sins. And through this, I learned to become a better unconditional lover of other people. I honestly would not be as much of a compassionate, empathetic person without trials, tribulations, and epic fails.

God made my stumbles part of the dance. My stumbles were actually essential to the beauty of the dance.

God made my stumbles part of the dance. My stumbles were actually essential to the beauty of the dance. My shortcomings slowly killed off my ego, which, in turn, allowed me to enter into the brokenness of those around me. Through my messes, I became a better unconditional and empathetic lover of others. Another gift of having my ego decrease was that I let other people into my life to love the real me. I helped them be unconditional friends to me.

And, my imperfections led me to be a better friend to other people. God changed my heart through my failures. I can see the beauty of others—flaws and all—and can let my ego go. This is all not about me. It is always about God and His love for everyone. My shortcomings in life will never have any power to diminish God's love for me or hinder my ability to show others that God does indeed love them. All I need to do is show others God's love and grace and let them and God do the rest. God will work with them to make their stumbles part of their dance. Just as I have to go to God to have Him change me, others need to do the same. I cannot change or control others. They do that through their relationship with their Creator. (By the way, this has taken a lot of time to learn this.) We cannot change others or stop them from stepping in front of the proverbial speeding train coming right at them. We love, and we let go.

By connecting with God through meditation and silence, I have begun to understand that no matter where I am in life, I can shout God's love from the mountaintop. God continues to heal all of the places in my life that cause me to falter. And you know what? The closer I get to God, the more faults I am able to see. I am much more aware of who I am. And all of this is okay. He continues to help me grow into my role as His daughter. We work on everything together.

So, this is where I feel as though my life has found some resolve. My proverbial dishes do not have a layer of muck on them anymore.

For all of you musicians (and music lovers out there), there is a concept of resolution. For example, the second to last note of a song is usually a note that feels like there needs to be another note for you to know that the song has ended. There needs to be movement from dissonance (an unstable sound) to consonance (a final, stable sound).

There was a comedy short by the Rowan Atkins character, Mr. Bean, that I always love to watch called "Mr. Bean Can't Stay Awake In Church."[14] It involves Mr. Bean in the front pew of a church singing the hymn "All Creatures of Our God and King." He did not really know the words, but always chimed in when they got to the "Alleluias" in the refrain. On the final refrain, the choir director really holds out the "Allelu" part of the last "Alleluia." Mr. Bean kept trying to sing the final "ia" to resolve the note and end the song. He tried about four times until the choir finally sang the last note. Mr. Bean looked so relieved when the note resolved, and the song ended.

Now that I have spent a lot of time getting closer to God and understanding that He wants my friendship more than anything, I feel as though I have some resolution. My life used to have no resolution, no understanding, no stability, and complete dissonance. Chasing after perfection and chasing after worldly things to fill my soul was like writing or singing a song with a note that does not resolve. Though the final note was apparent in my head, I could never actually hear it aloud. Not having the resolution caused stress and frustration, which led to anger, instability, and dissatisfaction. The feeling that something was wrong, but I did not know what was causing it.

On the flip side, when we are able to see that life is really about letting go, loving, and forgiving, we hear the song resolve. We don't struggle or go insane thinking that when we chase our worldly desires, there will never be a resolution.

---

14 John Howard Davies, *The Best Bits of Mr. Bean (1999; Universal City, CA:* Universal Studios Home Entertainment), DVD.

Each desire (even to be perfect) we pursue brings us disappointment. We blindly chase another worldly desire and end up in the same damn place—Grey Street—curled up in a fetal position, wondering whatever happened to our happiness.

We need to commit to actually believing God is who He says He is. We need to spend the time getting to know Him and be open to His healing. And my brothers and sisters, we need to take a little breather and give our poor imperfect selves a break. Be kind to yourself. Forgive yourself. Learn and grow. Your imperfections are driving you toward God.

And, as the Star Wars fighter would say during the attack on the Death Star: "Stay on Target."[15]

So, what does this look like every day?

For me, my feet hit the floor every morning and ask God, *So, what are we going to accomplish together today?* As cheesy as that might be, I really think that it is vital to continually remind myself that God and I work together through all things, every day. When we actually believe in God's Word, we believe that He really loves us and can develop a strong bond with Him. He is my biggest fan. We can invite Him into every second of our day to have every part of our imperfect life work to bring His goodness and love into the world. Our stumbles are part of the dance. Our imperfection does serve Him perfectly.

We are painting my life together in broad daylight. My experience in heaven has already started with my Savior. When I die, I will simply continue the relationship that I have with Him. This is truly my heaven on earth.

We are all called to live a life of love, and God has given us gifts to help us love and care for others. We must be willing to show up, though. We must be focused and brave. We must all stop running away and run toward Him.

---

15 George Lucas, *Star Wars Episode IV: A New Hope* (1977; Los Angeles, CA: Twentieth Century Fox Video, 2006), DVD.

I needed to stop running. I knew God called me to do so many things, and like so many before me, I thought there was no way that I would be able to do what I thought I was called to do. And I was in good company. Moses did not believe he was a good enough speaker (and lest we not forget, he killed someone). *"But Moses said to the Lord, "O my Lord, I have never been eloquent, neither in the past nor even now that you have spoken to your servant; but I am slow of speech and slow of tongue"* (Exodus 4:10). Jonah did not want to go to Nineveh and took off in another direction until a whale ultimately swallowed him before he accepted his mission. *"Go at once to Nineveh, that great city, and cry out against it; for their wickedness has come up before me." But Jonah set out to flee to Tarshish from the presence of the Lord ..."* (Jonah 1:2-3).

We can all do what we were called to do, no matter our strengths and our weaknesses. God can use them both in surprising ways. All we need to do is trust that God is who He says He is and will show up to show us the best of who we are. I think we all (including myself) forget just how powerful that God is and need to put things in His hands instead of cowering in fear and relying on ourselves. He is doing the work. Let's get out of our own way. We are God's work of art. The more I decrease, the more He can increase.

Another benefit I enjoy when I have God by my side every day is that my decisions and my foundation come from Him. I do not feel the pressure to change who I am due to the people around me. I am who I am, and God has given me the strength to be His disciple. People can make fun of me all they want and mock me or tell me I am crazy and exclude me from social circles. It really does not matter. I am truly free. My happiness and peace come from inside me. The more that I develop my connection with God, the stronger and more courageous I become. It is empowering because my decisions give me control over my peace and happiness. Nothing can touch it.

So, I am more consistent for other people in the same way God is consistent for me. People around me can do whatever they want, and life can throw whatever it wants at me—it really does not matter anymore. My dance is my dance, and I do not have to worry about what everyone else is doing. My foundation is my constant. This allows me not only to love and accept myself more but also to love and accept everyone around me. For those I love, there is nothing they can do to make me love them more or less.

Not surprisingly, when we have an authentic relationship with God and fall into God's love and grace, we become more genuine people, accessible for others to love. Our egos decrease in size when we readily admit our shortcomings, limitations, and expansiveness. Only then can we give our blank canvas to God to be used for His Kingdom. "Be uniquely you. Stand out. Shine. Be colorful. The world needs your prismatic soul!"—Amy Leigh Mercree

Impact

Danger: What you are about to read might make you really upset with me. (I guess this is good that I put this at the end of the book!) I challenge you to hear me out on all of this. I truly believe that God is calling all of us to reflect on our impact on the world.

I may be totally out there, but I would like to challenge all of us here to continue our quests to know God as our friend and to be His best friends. He needs us to develop our relationships with Him and impact others around us. The world needs all of us, and we cannot remain hidden in the world, scared of the God who loves us so profoundly.

Unfortunately, we have gotten to the point where the world sees religious people as judgmental, hateful, and unforgiving. I am going to go out on a limb and say that we exude these characteristics to the world because this is how many of us who are religious feel about ourselves and God. Referring back to that survey I mentioned at the beginning of this book, only 23% of those who responded would classify their God as benevolent. Almost 75% would consider their God distant, critical, or authoritarian.

Hard truth: If we see God as distant, critical, or authoritarian, we are most likely showing that to the world. If we think God is critical of us, we will be critical of others. If we feel God is distant, we will be distant from others or simply not think that God cares enough for us, so why should we put in the time to care for others? If God is authoritarian, then we will probably believe the religious experience is about control and power.

And of course, everyone is so focused on all spiritual and religious people being perfect that they claim we are hypocrites when we sin. But we are not hypocrites—we are imperfect. Our religion is not about how awesome we are as individuals; it is about the unconditional love of God and our constant striving to tap into this love so that our wounds are healed. I hate to admit it, but we created this *hypocrite monster* ourselves. We expect ourselves and others to be perfect. This is illogical and impossible. The only thing that we might be hypocritical about is saying that God loves us unconditionally and not really believing it ourselves. I admit I was a hypocrite about that, and I needed to change. This was a big ouch for me to confess.

> The only thing that we might be hypocritical about is saying that God loves us unconditionally and not really believing it ourselves.

We can see people's obsessiveness with perfection all around us. Brene Brown, a professional researcher, became popular with her research on guilt and shame. We have become a shame and guilt-filled society so much so it paralyzes us, especially many of us who believe in God. He can take all of this away from us if we let Him. He does not want us all beating ourselves up down here and saying how unworthy we are. That does not make the world a better place.

Showing God's love to ourselves and others makes the world a better place.

It is not our world to change. It is God's world to change. We cannot positively change the world solely on our own. We need to be the vessels God uses and get out of His way. We have to believe what God has to offer is better than what we have to offer because, quite frankly, it is. God can change the world through us if we let Him.

What if we all felt God's love and believed His Word and knew we were loved and forgiven and usable by God to change ourselves and help others? What if we accepted that God could change us and others and wants to help us in our pain? He wants to touch us where there is so much anguish, shame, guilt, embarrassment, fear, and confusion. What if we all did not sell our powerful God short and followed Him with confidence?

If we love the Lord, we owe it to Him to work with Him in our lives. We owe it to Him to accept His love, forgiveness, and mercy—and spread the Good News all over the world. But we cannot do this if we do not believe it ourselves.

The world needs us to believe, trust, and love God. God needs us to believe, trust, and love Him. The world is hurting. I do not need to convince anyone of that. There is violence, depression, anxiety, drug addictions, food addictions, suicides, loneliness, and much more. We are in a position to heal all of this together, and we need to start with letting God restore each and every one of us.

I challenge all of us to turn the tide on how God is viewed and religion is perceived worldwide. We need to feel loved, then we can love everyone else and accept them as-is into our churches and our lives. Our pain has the potential to save and heal others.

We are not new creatures without sin, but we are new creatures in Christ who have been reconciled to God. It *never* says we stopped being sinners. We are ambassadors for Christ and continue His work. What a load off! We never have to be perfect in God's eyes because we already are. Christ has made us beautiful. Our reconciliation to God allows us to focus on being Christ's disciples, bringing love to other people, and embracing this freedom. We should not wallow anymore in shame and fear, only love. This should be such a peaceful and empowering thought to all of us. We can rest in the Lord. He is Love.

If we as Jesus followers (The Prince of Peace, Wonderful Counselor, Lord of Life, Lord of All, Savior of the World) cannot feel this love of God, I am sorry to say there is something significantly wrong. I am not judging here. I have been there myself, so I know what it is like to feel unworthy of God's love.

But the beauty is that we can fix this with some spiritual focus and willingness to create change in ourselves. The world is waiting for all of us. It is waiting for us as the writers, musicians, health professionals, sports professionals, IT gurus, business people, ministers, moms, dads, kids, actors—everyone. The world is waiting for us to show up with our Creator's love and stop the chaos and sadness.

Just like Jesus chose His imperfect group of friends, He chose all of us. Our lives are wicked good and God awe-full. God will take our imperfections, heal them, and make these stumbles part of the graceful dance of His creation.

Our imperfections and missteps allow God to work His perfect plan in us. We just all need to have the courage to dance!

Be Still

Let Him be wildly in love with you

Let yourself be madly in love with Him

Take a deep breath

Live your life *with* God

And don't ever let your stumbles stop
you from dancing

Five Things You Can Do
Right Now

1. Honestly evaluate your friendship with God. Relationships are only enhanced by taking a genuine look at where you are and then building from there.

2. Challenge yourself to believe God is who He says He is: unconditionally loving and forgiving. Take this gift from God, and run with it!

3. Find time every day to pray but also to sit in silence and give yourself the gift of *listening* to God.

4. Spend time writing down the gifts that God has given you and how you think you can use them to help others know the love of God.

5. Wake up every day knowing that you are co-creating your life with God. Remind yourself throughout the day that you are not alone—even in your darkness.

Reflection Questions

Chapter 1

1. What is the status of your relationship with God? Do you see God as benevolent, distant, critical, or authoritarian? (Seriously, you need to spend at least a few days thinking about this. It is crucial to be completely honest with yourself here.) Is it a comforting friendship where you feel loved, or do you feel inadequate and judged?

2. Knowing all your faults, would you be like Peter and run to Jesus and embrace Him? Do you expect Him to always welcome you with open arms?

3. Where is God on your list of priorities? Again, be honest with yourself here.

Chapter 2

1. Can you find anything positive about being imperfect? Does being imperfect drive you toward or away from God? Do you let him help you with your imperfections?

2. Are you caught up in the worthiness game? How does that make you feel on a daily basis?

3. Do you see pain as the root of most sin? Does this impact the way you empathize with yourself and with others who struggle?

4. Is the goal of your spiritual life to be in a relationship with God or to try and be perfect on your own? Is your goal life-giving?

Chapter 3

1. Do you trust God 100% and believe that He is who He says He is? Do you believe to your core that He loves you unconditionally, has forgiven your sins, wants to heal you and help you grow? (All-in, no doubts.) If not, why not?

2. Do you think you are a good friend to God? (Not is He a good friend to you, but you being His best friend.) Where do you see room for improvement?

3. Do you feel peaceful and free in your life? If yes, how were you able to find this peace and freedom? If not, what is hindering you?

Chapter 4

1. Which friend of God (or Jesus if you are Christian) do you relate to the most in the Bible? Why?

2. Why does God need you as a friend? What are your strengths, and how can you use these strengths to positively impact the world? What would happen if you hid your strengths from others in the world? How would they be negatively impacted?

3. Can you trust that it is your job to love people and open their hearts? And can you trust it is God's job to change them?

Chapter 5

1. How does perfect fear drive out love in your life? How does perfect love drive out the fear?

2. How has the pain in our life been the salvation for someone else?

3. What expectations/conditions do you have of God? Are they reasonable? Do these expectations negatively affect your relationship with Him?

4. Do you equate the blessings in your life with how good you have been and tie the tragedies with you being a horrible sinner somehow? If so, why? Where did you learn to attach events in life with God's level of love for you?

Chapter 6

1. Are you living your spiritual life and relationship with God through other people? Do you tend to listen to others and read their books instead of experiencing God on your own? If so, why?

2. There is a quote from Anthony DeMello, which states: "Love Springs from Awareness." What does this mean to you? Have you experienced this? If yes, how so?

3. Are you open to committing time to be silent with God? If so, when and where? Make a plan. What other methods of building your foundation with God are you drawn to (writing, contemplating, reading the Bible, etc.)?

Chapter 7

1. We are responsible for creating the palette we will use with God to *paint* our true selves. What are you willing to give him? Only your strengths? Only your weaknesses? A combination of both?

2. Close your eyes and think of you and your life. What colors come to mind? Are they bright? Are they dark? Is it a lot of grey? Why do you think you see yourself this way? How do you think God sees you?

3. Do you see God as your *Bob Ross?* Do you think He can redeem even your worst mistakes? If not, why not?

Chapter 8

1. Are you letting your light shine in the world, or are you hiding it under a bushel? If you are hiding, why?

2. How have your failures in life actually made you more empathetic and unconditional loving of other people?

3. Do you wake up every day and ask God what the two of you are going to be up to today, or do you feel as though you are on your own? Why?

4. How do you think religion is viewed in our society? Why is this? Do you tell people that God loves them unconditionally, but do not really believe it?

5. Are you ready to dance? If not, what is holding you back?

Recommended Resources

There are many books, videos, webinars, websites, prayer resources, etc., for growing your relationship with God. I know many of you are tapping into a lot of this information, so I am going to challenge you to put all of this aside every day and just be alone with God.

God and You

The only resources that truly matter.

About the Author

Roberta Bryer-King a bit of a Renaissance woman (which is elegant for saying scattered). Her varied interests have led her through careers as a semi-pro golfer, stockbroker, IT manager, anti-human trafficking advocate as well as a youth and young adult minister. She has enjoyed dabbling in a bit of everything: playing classical guitar, tinkering with painting and sketching, singing, hiking, mountain biking, playing a stint as a lead guitarist in a rock band, and even earning a spot in the Little League Softball World Series as a youth. She is so competitive at board games she really cannot play them, and literally "enjoys long walks on the beach." Throughout her life, she has been involved in helping herself and others grow closer to God through the amazing and the mundane.

Roberta struggled with believing that the Creator of the Universe was indeed very much in love with her—imperfections and all. After years of self-discovery, prayer, and meditation, God transformed her so she could finally fully experience His love—actually feel it. God's grace and peace were transferred from her head to her heart, making her on fire for others to feel the same way. She now can clearly see that God truly does make her stumbles part of the dance.

Roberta has a degree in her first love, theology, from the University of Notre Dame (Go Irish!) where she also received a second undergraduate degree in economics. Later, she earned an MBA from Regis University. In addition, she has also been blessed to grow her faith through the Ignatian Spiritual Exercises, spiritual direction, and faith-based retreats. She has lived up and down the East Coast and now lives just outside her hometown in Ohio with her husband, Jim, and three amazing sons: Alexi, Nikita, and Misha.

You can connect with Roberta at RobertaBryer-King.com

Keep Dancing!

Visit robertabryer-king.com to continue your journey with webinars, podcasts, meditations, and blog posts. Encourage your fellow imperfect friends and become more empathetic and loving. We are all on this journey together!

CPSIA information can be obtained
at www.ICGtesting.com
Printed in the USA
BVHW090858031220
594764BV00014B/336/J